12/
68

SMALL BEGINNINGS

BARBARA CURTIS

FOREWORD BY WILLIAM SEARS, M.D.

BROADMAN
&HOLMAN
PUBLISHERS

Nashville, Tennessee

SMALL BEGINNINGS

Published by Broadman & Holman Publishers, Nashville, Tennessee
Acquisitions & Development Editor: Vicki Crumpton
Interior Design and Typography: TF Designs, Mt. Juliet, Tennessee
Cover Photos: little boy, FPG, Ron Chapple; little girl,
FPG, John Terrence Turner; mom/toddler, Stockline, Mark Kozlowski
Cover Design: Left Coast Design, Inc., Portland, Oregon

4262-87
0-8054-6287-2

Dewey Decimal Classification: 649
Subject Heading: PARENTING / CHILD REARING
Library of Congress Card Catalog Number: 96-30264

Unless otherwise noted, Scripture quotations are from the Holy Bible, New International Version, copyright © 1973, 1978, 1984 by International Bible Society.

Library of Congress Cataloging-in-Publication Data
Curtis, Barbara, 1948–
    Small beginnings : first steps to prepare your child for lifelong learning / Barbara Curtis
        p.   cm.
    Includes bibliographical references.
    ISBN 0-8054-6287-2
    1. Toddlers—Care. 2. Child rearing—Religious aspects. 3. Child development—Religious aspects. I. Title.
HQ769.C965   1997
649'.1—dc20

96-30264
CIP

97 98 99 00 01 5 4 3 2

To my children:
Samantha, Jasmine, Joshua,
Matthew, Benjamin, Zachary,
Sophia, Jonathan, Madeleine,
Jesse, and Daniel—

who, along with my students,
taught me more about children
than books or teachers ever could.

And to my husband, Tripp,
who made it all possible.

And whoever welcomes a little child like this
in my name welcomes me.
Matthew 18:5

Contents

Acknowledgments

More than thirty years ago, my high school English teacher predicted I would someday be a professional writer, but I remembered that only two years ago when I finally began to write. It took a lot of living to get me here.

Now I find myself in the strange predicament of raising a multitude of young children (nine under age thirteen), squeezing hours here and there to finish this project. But, as you will see, if I didn't have the life God has given me, I would have nothing to say.

If I learned a lot before I began to write, I have learned more since. The lessons that mean the most are those concerning the love and kindness of those around me.

I have learned that my husband, Tripp—though I don't often find the words or time to tell him—is a wonderfully considerate man. I will never forget the fresh gardenias he placed by my computer so I could enjoy their fragrance as I wrote; nor the special times he made for our children as I put the finishing touches on this book.

I have learned that my children have actually absorbed much of what I've taught them, as they have supported and encouraged me—with lots of help and hugs. This book could not have been written without the devoted assistance of Jasmine, my second daughter, who took care of the house, drove children here and there, brought me coffee, salads, and conversation to sustain me.

I was blessed to find a school to which I could briefly entrust the education of my children. Knowing the joy and responsibility of home-schooling, I feel especially indebted to their teachers: Sharon Losey, Candy Macias, Sue Casteel, and Kimberly Sutton.

I am grateful to Mount Hermon for the yearly writer's conferences. Attending one was the first step I took when I felt the call to write. Beyond a doubt, I never could have reached this point without the education I received and the people I met there.

Special thanks to Elaine Wright Colvin, who clearly communicated the practical knowledge I needed to go beyond having a message to making sure it would be heard. And hugs to my high-tech son-in-law, Kip Walraven, who spent hours working to improve the relationship between me and my computer.

I am grateful for many supportive friends, especially Robin Strom, who is an expert at unconditional love, and Audrey Kohout, who has a gift for speaking into my life at crucial times. Thanks to Debbie Sharpe, who faithfully pored over my finished manuscript and offered ideas for further improvement.

Heartfelt thanks to Vicki Crumpton, my editor, and Broadman & Holman, my publisher, for believing in me. When Vicki called to tell me a contract was on its way, I felt like Sally Field, who accepted her Academy Award bubbling like a little girl, "You like me. You really like me!"

Finally: For nine years, not a day has passed when I haven't remembered with a smile the man most responsible for our family's peace and stability. It is only appropriate that I acknowledge James Dobson. Through his "Focus on the Family" radio ministry, Tripp and I were brought to a place where we realized we needed Jesus Christ in our lives. And Jesus is an essential part of the parents we have become. From both of us, then, thank you, Dr. Dobson.

Thanks as well to Dennis and Barbara Rainey and Family Life Ministry for sharing the Four Spiritual Laws and showing us how to build our family on God's foundation. As Dennis is always the first to say, "We appreciate you!"

Novato, California
January 1997

Foreword

❦

The useful advice Barbara Curtis gives in this book reflects the wisdom found in Proverbs, "Train up a child the way he should go and when he is old he will not depart." Key to this age-old parenting wisdom is to discover the child's natural bent, which way he should go and which parenting style is going to work for each individual child.

As a father of eight, one of the first lessons I learned about parenting is that to truly be an authority figure in my home, I had to learn how to get behind the eyes of my children and see things from their viewpoint—to understand why they behave the way they do—so I could then shape their behavior in the direction I wanted them to go. The information Barbara gives in this book helps parents achieve the two early goals of parenting: to know your child and to help your child feel right. Throughout this book, there are useful tools to help parents get to know their child—to get behind the eyes of their child—and to be able to read their child's behavior in a way that they can channel the child's behavior toward a useful purpose.

Small Beginnings is based on a very important principle of child development: the role of a facilitator in helping a child develop to his maximum potential. At each stage of development a child needs significant people who care about him and whom he cares about. These people act as facilitators, helping the child learn how to conduct himself in the world. A facilitator is like a consultant, a trusted authority figure who provides emotional refueling to the child, a person to lean on who helps the child both develop his skills and take advantage of the resources around him with a view toward becoming self-sufficient. Facilitators don't tell the child what to do, they help the child learn what to do. The facilitator watches for teachable moments and takes advantage of them.

Raising a child can bring out the best and the worst in parents. In *Small Beginnings* Barbara Curtis gives parents the tools to help them bring out the best in their child and the best in themselves. Remember, God would not have given you the privilege of raising a child without also giving you the tools to raise a godly child. This book will help you discover your God-given abilities so that you can help your child better discover his. This book portrays the biblical model of parenting: experienced parents sharing their wisdom with new parents. Certainly Barbara Curtis, mother of eleven, has a lot of wisdom to share.

William Sears, coauthor of *The Baby Book*

Part One
On Your Mark!

Five Strategies for Joyful Parenting

You have toddlers in your life, little bundles of energy and demands who sometimes make you wish your name was anything but Mom. Demolition Derby wannabe's wailing because of a two-minute pit stop for fresh diapers. Near-disasters you barely miss tripping over several times each day. (I tripped over one of my own toddlers once—while flying a kite—and wore a cast for a few months to remind me never to take for granted the space around my ankles.)

Toddlers are the stuff of which soap manufacturers' dreams are made—you know because since having them, you've spent countless hours with stains and detergents. Or worse, days with soggy carpets and industrial fans. One sunny afternoon, I had settled my older toddlers with a video so I could bathe Zachary, at that time our newest addition, in peace. Of course, the doorbell rang. Grabbing a towel, I bundled the baby, raced down the stairs, then slipped and almost fell head over heels as my feet hit the tile floor in the foyer. Words will never describe the shock as I caught my balance and realized that what had nearly tumbled the baby and me was a couple inches of water—on the first floor of our home. The salesman at the open front door was gaping with me at my son Benjamin, clad only in a diaper and a smile. In Ben's hand was the garden hose, going full blast. My industrious two-year-old had somehow decided to water the house, and from his expression it was clear that he thought it had been a job well done.

Who can fathom the mind of a two-year-old? Or a three-year-old? And what if you have one of each? Just running around after toddlers squeezes more ounces of energy than you ever imagined could be squeezed from the human body.

Still a certain smile can make you remember why you had them, maybe even wish you had a few more. On a good day you may feel that you preside over the greatest treasure on earth. Other days you feel like screaming. I know because as a mother of eleven and as an experienced Montessori teacher, I have had toddlers in my life for twenty-six years. As a teacher and a mother, I share these moments too.

Let's face it: There's a lot about them (and maybe a little about ourselves) we'd like to change. A good cry, a hurried prayer, a phone call from a friend, a long hot bath—all can help you cope. But take it from one who's been there—and stayed a lot longer than most!—there are practical ways as well to bring out the best in toddlers. That's what *Small Beginnings* is all about.

A Little about Me

Twenty-some years ago, with college and my Montessori training behind me,[1] I thought my education was complete. I never dreamed it had only begun. Over the years ahead, I discovered so much more as I taught in different classrooms. My understanding of children continued to grow as I taught in schools on the east coast and the west, in inner-city and suburban settings. My students—coming from so many different cultures and backgrounds—challenged my everyday assumptions and verified the universality of the principles and techniques which were part of my training.

Still, I had no idea that my final and most significant training would ultimately be in my own home with my own children. Until 1983, I was a normal mother of two. But in the last thirteen years, our family has grown to a total of eleven children (nine by birth, two by adoption)—qualifying me as no longer quite normal, I guess. In 1987 (presumably in answer to my prayer to become a better parent!), I became a Christian.

If all these things were mixed together to produce a distinct perspective on parenting toddlers, the end result was refined in an old but serviceable oven: homeschooling. For five years, I have taught my children at home, putting what I have learned into practice while also being pregnant, giving birth, and nursing babies. It was this unique blend of my education, Montessori teaching experience, God's grace, and hands-on family life that gave birth to *Small Beginnings*.

About the Book

Many people have been curious about our family. How could I teach the elementary age children with so many toddlers buzzing around? How did I get anything done? And how did I keep from going crazy? My *Small Beginnings* workshops began as a way to share my answers to their questions.

Mothers came seeking ways to keep their toddlers out of their hair. They went home with something more positive: a vision for where their toddlers were going and how to best get them there.

This book gives you an opportunity to catch this vision. I share with you the tears and triumphs involved in the daily adventure of parenting toddlers. But there is more I want to share. I believe that God has built some wonderful potentials into our children, potentials which will enable them to become better learners wherever they go to school—home, public, or private. And looking farther into the future (which is something that can keep you going when times get tough), your early understanding of these potentials will help you guide them to finally become men and women of strong character.

Specifically, this book will:

- 🍎 give you insight into the way toddlers see their world,

- 🍎 outline simple, specific, attainable goals for your toddler's development,

- 🍎 provide keys that will unlock your child's potential to become a capable student as he grows older, and

- 🍎 share some special learning materials you can create yourself to bring out the best in your toddler.

At the Start Line

Along the way, you will probably do some changing yourself. My children have been the greatest instrument of change in my own life. That's why I've structured this book in sections titled, "On Your Mark!" "Get Set!" and "Go!"

Several times in the New Testament the Christian life is compared to running a race. Those writers may not have been thinking specifically of us, but we parents know exactly what they meant. Sometimes we're so out of breath we don't know if we'll make it to bedtime, much less the finish line.

Raising toddlers is more like a marathon than a 100-yard dash. What are the secrets to finishing the race?

First, successful distance runners take the long view, see the big picture; that is, they familiarize themselves with the course in advance. They know exactly where they're headed and how to make it to the finish.

When they are discouraged, they remind themselves of crossing the finish line. They focus on that burst of triumph they will feel. In a long race, though runners cannot see it, their eyes are still on the goal.

Sometimes they make mistakes. But when a runner's step falters—at the start, in the middle, even toward the end—

he keeps on going. He might even come back stronger. In other words, a mistake is not enough to ruin the rest of the race and perhaps may be the push he needs to finish well.

Finally, for the best runners, coming in first may be the goal, but more important is the satisfaction of knowing they ran their best race. Like Eric Lidell, the 1924 Olympic champion portrayed in *Chariots of Fire*, the best runners find joy not so much in winning, but in being stretched to give their best. Eric ran to please the Lord: "When I run, I feel His pleasure."

Now, apply these principles to parenting:

- ❦ Get the big picture.
- ❦ Keep your eyes on the goal.
- ❦ Acknowledge mistakes, but keep moving forward.
- ❦ Bring your best to each moment.

Above all else, before running the race, the best athletes are prepared and conditioned—physically and mentally as well. To do our best, we parents need to be too.

So that's where *Small Beginnings* will begin—with our own conditioning. Let's see how we can run our own race filled with purpose and joy. After all, raising children may be the most demanding marathon of all.

Take it from one who knows!

Chapter One

Observe: Prime-Time Viewing

"What does this monkey have to do with teaching?" I grumbled to myself. Though it was one o'clock in the afternoon, the sky was bleak and gray, and the concrete zoo bench was sending a night-like chill through my body. With one hand stuffed in my jacket pocket, I clenched my pen resentfully and stared at the gibbon picking through the banana peels and apple chunks littering the floor of his cage.

How was I going to make it through two hours with this hairy specimen? And two hours tomorrow? What if it rained? Why was I here anyway? And what would the staff dream up for my next assignment? I was supposed to be studying to become a teacher, not a zoologist!

Looking back now after more than twenty years of teaching and living with children, I see a lot of the child in that young teaching student. The feelings recalled so vividly from that day have given me an unforgettable glimpse into the heart of the four-year-old.

Haven't each of us been frustrated by the child who becomes momentarily unteachable, face squinched and body locked in the I-already-know-how-to-do-it stance that must be softened before anything can break through?

That day in front of the animal cage I may have been twenty-something on the outside, but inside my attitude was more that of a know-it-already three-year-old.

So zealous had I been about my calling as a teacher that after two years of course overloads in college, I had finally persuaded the governing board at the Montessori Institute in Washington, D. C., to make an exception and waive the degree requirement just for me. At last a teaching student, I was now more eager than ever to learn how to teach. And yet, our first assignment had nothing to do with children: We were to go to the zoo, choose an animal, observe it for two-hour sessions, and record our observations. Down to the last detail. You can imagine how well this sat with my hasty, hurried heart!

The gibbon stared impassively at the bench next to mine as though to convince me I wasn't really there.

"He sat motionless," I wrote and punched the period defiantly.

He picked up a tidbit and absentmindedly tasted it. His posture reminded me of a sculpture—so calm and composed.

I was straining for specific observations, thinking these would be the longest two hours of my life. Yet, finally I gave myself up to the task in resignation.

The next thing I knew, it had begun to rain and I was hurriedly cramming my notebook and pen in my backpack and dashing for cover. After looking at my watch, I was startled to realize that I had actually been recording observations for two and a half hours!

What I learned from my hours at the zoo that gray day was more than I could ever learn from books or classrooms.

First I learned a lesson in humility. My teachers really did know what I needed. Of course they knew I wasn't planning on zoology as a career, but they understood something I had yet to learn—to give my best to children, I would need to start by seeing them clearly. I had to learn to observe.

My year at the institute would include hundreds of hours and pages of assigned observation of children—individually and in groups—in classrooms throughout metropolitan Washington. My training was rigorous, but it taught me first-hand what a powerful tool observation is for an educator.

Now I'm a mother. But through the years, I've become even more convinced that observation is a vital skill for parents in learning what makes their children tick.

Observation is the starting point for parents in releasing our children's God-given potential.

In fact, observation is the starting point for parents in releasing our children's God-given potential. How many times are we advised in Scripture to consider? Consider the lilies, consider the ravens, or the all-encompassing, "Stop and consider God's wonders" (Job 37:14).

We need to consider our children. We need to stop, look, and listen to them as they go about their small pursuits. If God uses the lilies and the ravens to teach us the things He wants us to know, I am convinced He can use our children as well.

Observation takes time and commitment and purpose. And unlike teaching students, we parents rarely have the luxury of sitting for a couple hours simply watching our children.

Seize opportunities when you can. While you're busy with dishes and your child is absorbed in emptying the cabinets, take a few moments to watch him carefully, to focus on the details that make him uniquely the person he is. Ask God to help you see your child the way He sees him.

Two-minute snatches grabbed here and there through-out the day, if done on a regular basis, can be enough to es-tablish a habit of observation. Soon you'll have the skill of a professional educator in observing your particular child.

Let me count for you the benefits:

🐛 You will grow in the knowledge of and love for your children.

🐛 You will come to understand not only how your chil-dren fit into general schemes of development, but also their unique patterns.

🐛 You will know the minute they are ready to learn some-thing new, or when they need a new angle on learning something old.

🐛 You will gain insight into details of behavior that might otherwise threaten to drive you crazy.

🐛 You will see clearly your children's strengths and weak-nesses. You will know exactly how to pray for them.

Being a committed observer also helps you avoid the trap of labeling a child, then failing to notice when the label no longer fits. Careful observation will alert you to the slightest shifts and changes in his behavior, attitude, and abilities. This gives your child more room to grow and change. It also keeps your prayers fresh and up to the minute, rejoicing and thanking God for each small improvement, each little victory.

My daughter Sophia, at three, had a whine like nails on chalkboard—it set my teeth on edge. Together we built a useless pattern: At the first few notes of her whining, I would stop listening. Completely ignoring her question, I'd say, "I don't listen to whining." Then, try as she might, she would be too frustrated to produce anything better. I was begin-ning to fear that she might someday leave for college with-out ever conquering The Dreaded Whine!

But I found a special time to talk to her about whining to let her know how unappealing it was and how it made people around her feel.[1] We practiced saying things with a whine and without. Then we prayed together that God would help her with this problem. After all, children's problems are as big to them as our problems are to us. They need all the help they can get.

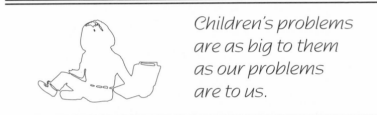

Children's problems are as big to them as our problems are to us.

The next time Sophia started to whine, I felt my habitual response on the tip of my tongue. But then I caught myself. Because I had been observing Sophia closely, my ears had become sensitive enough to detect an ever-so-slight difference in her tone. She really was trying her best not to whine! Wanting to focus on and encourage her progress, I gave her a hug.

"Thank you for not whining!" I said encouragingly.

Now her voice dropped a few more notches in the direction of normal as she told me what was on her mind.

Think of what happens when you decide to break a bad habit. Sometimes the break is dramatic, but more often, change comes in increments—a little at a time. When this happens with our children, we need to acknowledge their efforts.

At moments like the one above, I am grateful I was taught to observe. I can assure you that you, too, will find great rewards from adding this special tool to your parenting skills.

Am I making too much of the potential of observation as a teaching tool? I think not. Jesus had a keen eye for His culture, and the power of His parables relied on His asking His listeners to observe the behavior of everyday people in everyday situations. In this way their understanding would be increased.

Watch your child carefully, especially when he is unaware of your eyes. How does he like to sit? What does he like to do? What evokes his power of concentration? Does he need to slow down or to speed up? Would it help if he held his crayon differently or placed his coloring book at a different angle? What frustrates him, distracts him, makes him worry? What produces a look of accomplishment, a sigh of satisfaction? What is his biggest problem? What brings out his best? Is he ready for a challenge? What can you do to take him to the next level?

In addition to all its other benefits, I believe that careful consideration actually nurtures feelings of tenderness in the observer for the observed. Before your married life was filled with children and other distractions, did you ever grow tired of looking into your spouse's eyes? Think of the hours you spent gazing at your first child and bonding with him.

That's why it's important to forget the messes and the madness whenever you can. Capture as many moments as possible to observe each of your children—what they're doing, and when, where, why, and how. Remember to ask God to help you see what He needs you to see.

Consider these moments carefully and you will know your children well.

Chapter Two

Understand: It's *Not* a Small World

"Daddy, your legs are tall as trees. And I can't keep up with runny trees!"

Zachary was almost three when he captured his dad's attention with this word picture of trees running. The entire family was grateful the big man got the point and we could catch our breath. Tripp is so tall that when he's tilting full steam ahead, I have a hard time keeping up with him myself. From the children's point of view, the task is impossible—unless their father takes their little legs into account.

Proportionately speaking, our toddlers see us from the same perspective with which we would gaze up at someone on five-foot stilts! Imagine the effect at church, in the supermarket, or any place where grownups congregate. Next time you have a gathering of adults, try sitting on the floor for a real taste of how the waist-high-and-under group sees us. How strange it must seem to them to be surrounded by our legs! And how it must hurt their necks! All that looking up and pulling on skirts and pant legs. How hard they work trying to cope with the out-of-proportion world in which they live. No wonder they're so worn out at the end of the day!

My point is this: In our busy lives, with all the important, grown-up things grabbing our attention, how often do we look around to see the world our children see?

Probably not often at all. As adults, we have put away childish things. And rightly so—otherwise there'd be no cars or computers or hospitals or libraries. But in putting away childish things, most of us have forgotten what it feels like to be a child.

The result: Though we occupy the same planet, live in the same town, share the same home, move through the same rooms, our worlds are worlds apart. The distance in the perspectives from which we see things creates constant friction in our relationships with children.

It's up to us to bridge the gap; and, with a little creative thinking and remembering, it is very possible. To understand children, we first need to step into their very small shoes, grasp unwieldy objects with their little hands, cope with the king-sized obstacles they encounter, and process it all with their unsophisticated (yet delightful) way of thinking. See things with *their* eyes; hear with *their* ears.

Ever hear things differently than your child? If there's a toddler in your life, you've undoubtedly experienced something like the following: The Curtis family had watched Daddy and big brothers Joshua and Matthew put up the Christmas tree. Now Daddy was struggling (as usual) with the lights while the children waited not-so-patiently, jiggling boxes of ornaments waiting to be hung.[1]

Impatience being in direct proportion to fewer years, that year Sophia was having the hardest time.

"Are we almost ready, Daddy? Can't we just hang one, Daddy?"

"Not yet, Sophia. Just give me a few more minutes," Tripp replied patiently. But his patience wore thin after a few more "Daddy, plee-eeases."

"Sophia, hold your horses!" Daddy suddenly said, with exasperation.

Sophia sat bewildered, looking at the ornaments in front of her. I knew what was coming.

Finally, looking up with a puzzled expression, she said, "But, Daddy, I don't have any horses!"

The room filled with laughter from older brothers and sisters, leaving Sophia more puzzled than ever. Her dad had asked her to hold the horses, and she didn't have a clue where to find them!

We shouldn't take anything for granted with children. In language, children are very practical; they take things literally. To avoid misunderstandings, we have to hear it their way. No ironic twist, no cliché, no figure of speech is safe!

In other areas, the same holds true. With our own childhoods far behind, it does not come naturally to see things from the perspective of children. But our homes will run more smoothly when we make an effort to understand the daily struggles children face just climbing up to their chairs at the table or putting on their clothes with all the sleeves, legs, and buttons in the right places.

How often do we lose patience with children, forgetting that though we occupy the same territory, our experiences are vastly different? How frustrating it must be for them when we don't understand that the tasks we find so simple and automatic are complex and time-consuming to them.

Yet, adults who spend their days with children—parents and teachers alike—have at our disposal the greatest teacher's aid there is: *Do unto others as you would have them do unto you.*

The Golden Rule is more than a code of morality for our adult relationships—it applies to how we live in families and how we treat our children as well. Applied to parenthood, it means we treat children with dignity, with respect for their limitations. While exercising authority, we do all we can to avoid demeaning or belittling them. We are courteous and considerate. We remember to put ourselves in their place, to try to understand the difficulties they face, to see the world through their eyes.

"But you are so patient. That's why God gave you such a large family. I could never have so many children—I just don't have the patience myself." I hear remarks like this wherever I go.

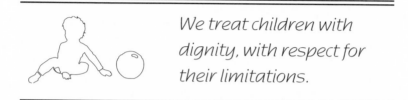

We treat children with dignity, with respect for their limitations.

I am grateful to be a patient person. Life is easier when your feathers remain mostly unruffled. But, I must confess, I don't deserve the credit for my patience. The glory has never been mine.

Sometimes I wish I wore a banner to proclaim that I started the same as everyone else: I used to be a normal person. But God gave me many children, and through the years I have become patient as a result of having and living with them.[2]

Let's face it: We all could use more understanding, more patience in every area of our lives—on the freeway, in crowded grocery aisles, in long lines at the post office. Having a lot of children seems to be one way to develop the kind of patience that will sail you through the day-to-day difficulties that still torment the less encumbered. However, no one needs to have eleven children to develop patience.

The first step is to recognize patience as a worthwhile and attainable goal. If you've been looking at the world as made up of two kinds of people, the patient and the not-so, realize that anyone can become more patient with willingness and prayer.

I must confess that finding quiet time has been my greatest struggle, but I have managed through the years of diapers and laundry to spend a lot of time reflecting on the qualities of Jesus while going about my daily tasks. One reason I don't mind housework is that it frees my mind for greener pastures and stiller waters, like the ones David spoke of in Psalm 23.

Patience is one of the qualities I have to think about frequently. Jesus modeled patience for us so well. The people who tried His patience were not those who made mistakes, but those who laid heavy burdens on others, expecting more from them than their Heavenly Father would.

When I think of how patient God has been with me through some of my stubborn times, I want to do my best to give my own children no less.

Patience is the result of observing, loving, and learning about our children. It is ultimately the result of learning to serve to the best of our ability and of being willing to change. The first step in this process is to see the world through their eyes. And the first place we turn our gaze is on ourselves.

Chapter Three

Model: Little Mirrors

"Joshua, that's the third bowl of cereal you've spilled this week!" My first son's shoulders slumped at my shrill tone of voice. I could see he felt like a failure.

That wasn't how I wanted him to feel. I just couldn't understand why he seemed unable to carry his cereal bowl from the kitchen counter to the table without making a mess.

"Next time, use two hands!" Now I felt like a failure as well. Even as I jerked a towel from the drawer and impatiently started cleaning up, I knew I was the one in the wrong.

Have you ever been upset over spilt milk? Or apple juice, Cheerios, paint, or bubbles? Ever felt your temper rise—whether you lost or kept it—when a dish was broken or mud was tracked in? Children's carelessness is a constant source of frustration to us.

But one thing children are long on is forgiveness. Josh was off on some adventure, with the spilt cereal and my unkindness long behind him, while I was still mulling over the situation in my own prayer closet—the laundry room.

My teacher training had taught me never to undermine my students' confidence if I wanted them to succeed. Why should it be any different with my own children? Didn't

I want the best for them? Why didn't it come naturally to apply time-tested teaching principles in my own home?

That morning I was convinced that the tools God had given me in my training as a teacher were not meant to be set aside when I became a mother; He would want me to use them now more than ever—in fact, maybe that's what they had been intended for all along!

This marked a turning point in my motherhood, as I made a covenant with God to put to use all that He had given me, while keeping my heart open and teachable.

Now the explanation for Joshua's kitchen clumsiness was clear. My mother's eyes couldn't see it, but my teacher's eyes could.

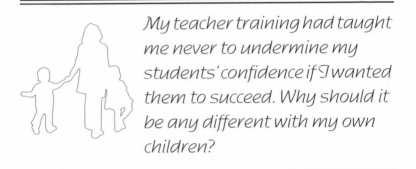

My teacher training had taught me never to undermine my students' confidence if I wanted them to succeed. Why should it be any different with my own children?

Throughout my training and in my years in the classroom, one guiding principle was modeling careful movement for our children—even exaggerating the precision needed for a particular task—to enable them to succeed.

Joshua was really my Little Mirror. If he was clumsy in the kitchen, it was because I should have realized that I could not habitually carry a cereal bowl with one hand while expecting him to carry it with two.

Children look up to us, literally and figuratively. Little ones, especially, are influenced by our slightest movements and gestures. How often have you been startled by an all-too-familiar mannerism unconsciously mimicked by someone half your height? It might have brought you amusement or shame, or a mixture of feelings.

When my two-year-old picks up the phone and nods and chatters to the dial tone, I am amused. But when my four-year-old daughter scolds her daddy in a certain style, I am brought up short by God's reminder that I am not always as kind as I should be myself. I try then to be grateful that God has given me so many Little Mirrors to show me how I can be better at what I do.

My son-in-law surprised himself one day. Having finished giving his eighteen-month-old son a bath, he bundled him in a towel and headed for the bedroom. Being an efficient kind of guy, he was planning three steps in advance. As he passed the living room he tossed a hairbrush over to the couch so he could sit and comb Timmy's curly red hair once he was diapered and pajamaed.

"Before the brush was out of my hand, I realized what a mistake I had made, but it was too late!" Kip later told me, I-can't-believe-myself written all over his face.

Sure enough, the minute Timmy was off the changing table, as his dad was gathering up the towel, the little guy darted into the living room, grabbed the brush, and gleefully threw it across the room like a Frisbee, just as his daddy had done.

Yes, they are our Little Mirrors.

Want a challenge? Take a day and carefully observe yourself. How do you move about your kitchen? Are you like a wasp in a whirlwind, darting from one distraction to another? Is setting the table a balancing act worthy of circus acrobats—a stack of plates in one hand, a tower of cups in the other? Is your mind on what you're doing or on what you're going to do?

When we become willing to see ourselves through our children's eyes, we begin to see how much we are at the root of their problems maneuvering through life. What happens when they are in a hurry, unconscious of what they are doing, or trying to do more than one thing at a time? More often than not, they fail; and we of little patience just can't seem to understand why they can't do such simple things right.

Children are born imitators. God made them that way for a reason: He wants them to model themselves after their parents. That is the surest way to build a foundation. What an awesome responsibility for us! We can't ask our children to stop imitating; instead, we can become worthy of imitation, even in the smallest details of our behavior.

Translated into everyday activity, this means we use as much concentration to do something as our children need to do it. When their eyes are present, we might spend more time than we ordinarily need to do the simple things. We can walk more slowly when we carry something. We can carry smaller amounts and use two hands. We can open and shut doors and drawers more carefully. We can tie their shoes as though it were the most absorbing activity in the world. We can try to do only one thing at a time and to be completely focused on the task at hand.

This discipline helps us appreciate the significance of the insignificant details that make up the fabric of our lives. Isn't it exciting to know that with just a little more attention to detail you can model tasks in ways that can help your children maximize their successes and minimize their messes?

So far we've talked about the physical, our outer selves, the things we do that are easy to see. There's an equally significant part of who we are that we need to look at as well.

What's beneath the surface? Our attitudes and responses—these need to be considered if we are to set our children on the path to successful living. This will be the focus of the next chapter.

In Titus 2:7, Paul tells us, "In everything set them an example by doing what is good." Don't underestimate the significance of the little things. Think of it as behind-the-scenes education, every bit as important as the math and language lessons your children will receive in years to come.

Well worth the investment, and good for you too.

Chapter Four

Change: Bring Out the Best

Ouch! Sometimes it hurts! But to be the best we can be—the parents God intended for our children—we start with our hearts.

We can't deny what a powerful influence our actions have on those of our children. Likewise, and perhaps even more so, our attitudes are reflected in theirs. For better or worse, in our strengths and in our weaknesses, they are our Little Mirrors.

Twenty years ago, I had a powerful lesson in how adults are responsible for their children's likes and dislikes. As a teacher on staff in an inner-city school in Washington, D. C., 90 percent of my students came from homes with incomes below the poverty level. Entering the school at age two and a half with few language or social skills, they were like absorbent sponges, eagerly soaking up whatever was placed before them. They were wonderful, delightful, and challenging children!

As one of our many efforts to enrich the environment, we enlisted in a visiting pet program. Each week, an animal van delivered three animal cages, one for each class. Inside were the special visitors—birds one week, rodents the second, and so on.

This was exciting for the children, many of whom had never had any exposure to animals. They thoroughly enjoyed the parakeet the first week and the hamster the next.

But unfortunately, the teachers and assistants were not sure how much they could enjoy any of it. We had been in a state of panic from the moment the administrator had handed us the schedule. You see, the hamster and the bird were fine, but on the third week things would be different— very different.

That was reptile week, the week when each classroom would be receiving a snake as its pet-of-the-week. We teachers spent a great deal of time discussing our apprehension, with many avowals from those who swore that they would never go near "those things."

The fateful day came. To allow them to acclimate to the new surroundings as peacefully as possible, the animals were delivered on Friday afternoons to spend a quiet weekend before the Monday morning ado. Three rather small garter snakes in three cages were waiting in the office for three head teachers to carry to our respective classrooms.

Full of disgust, I brought mine down the hall and set it on the counter just inside the door. Yucccck!

A city girl, I never had been this close to a snake and was not at all thrilled with the idea of having it in my classroom. However, there was a tension within me between my own aversion and the challenge my feelings presented. After all, I had been assured that the snake was harmless and that the children would be able to enjoy holding it. It didn't seem right to be so in bondage to my fears.

I braced myself and, lifting the screen top, gingerly touched, then lifted the little snake from its resting place on a piece of gnarled wood. I was surprised to feel how smooth his skin was, not at all as I had expected. He (or she) seemed somewhat nervous, but as I remained very still and grew a little calmer myself, so did he. By the time I put him back, I knew in my heart I was ready for Monday morning.

> *No matter what*
> *your actions are,*
> *your children will read*
> *your heart; and that is*
> *the heart theirs*
> *will become.*

Monday came and so did circle time. After a careful demonstration of the importance of being calm while handling the snake, I allowed the children to pass him around. Not only did they respond well to the new visitor, but they also thoroughly enjoyed the challenge of learning how to make him comfortable by being calm themselves. By the time he was returned to his cage, our snake had found a place in our classroom's heart.

But, oh, how surprised we were on the playground that day! While my students were bubbling with excitement about our pet of the week, the children from the other classes were aghast to hear that we had actually touched it. Their teachers, in not overcoming their own feelings of fear and disgust, had passed on their negative feelings.

What a vivid picture of our Little Mirrors! And what an emphatic image of how powerful our attitudes are in the shaping of theirs. Though this was not a lesson on a specifically spiritual matter, this was an important spiritual lesson for me as a teacher and later as a mother.

From that experience, I learned the necessity of taking an honest look at my own limitations. There is double joy to be found in transcending limitations rather than passing them on.

How overwhelming and humbling that God has entrusted us with the awesome privilege of shaping our children to be the best they can be. But that carries with it the responsibility to be the best *we* can be.

There is no way around it: No matter what your actions are, your children will read your heart; and that is the heart theirs will become.

Here's another challenge: As you spend a day observing your actions, why not spend a few days observing your heart?

Prepare with prayer, asking God to illuminate those areas that stand between the children in your care and all that God has for them. Are there fears that are ready to be let go? Are there bad habits of the heart, unwholesome attitudes that have been there so long we have forgotten to think about changing them? For those of us who come from non-Christian or unloving backgrounds, it is imperative to be willing to leave no stone unturned in our self-observation. For those from secure Christian backgrounds, the struggle may have more to do with complacency or pride.

In His gentleness, God may reveal only a little at a time. We need only ask each day, "Create in me a clean heart," and He will continue to shape us as we shape the children He has entrusted to our care. In this way we will become more gentle, patient, and filled with joy each day.

Isn't it wonderful how God designed this to work? In learning to become better parents, we actually learn to be the best we can be.

Chapter Five

Be Encouraged:
In Quietness and Confidence

Some people travel around the world, perfect their golf stroke or their makeup, and float through rooms right out of the pages of *Architectural Digest.* Others of us raise children—a brave and often chaotic enterprise—dashing from doctor's appointment to Little League, clearing dinner dishes to make way for homework.

You may be reading this book with your first baby in your arms, just looking ahead to find out where you're going.

You may already have a toddler or two—maybe a baby as well. If so, your biggest accomplishment each day may be to get everyone to nap simultaneously so that you can get a little rest yourself. You may be reading this book in snatches, between diapers and feedings and picking up the house, a page—or even a paragraph—at a time. I've been there myself.

You may be a homeschool mom, facing the challenge of teaching older children while coping with little ones. I've been there too.

You may be a teacher, looking for ideas for your classroom. Or a grandmother, looking for a fresh approach to the newest additions to the family. I've been—well, let's face it, there aren't too many places I haven't been with children.

Right now—maybe only for a little while—you have toddlers in your life. You may be frustrated because these little ones seem unfocused, aimless, or distracted. Perhaps they are not able to choose or concentrate on an activity and seem overly dependent on you for direction. Wherever they go, they leave a trail of clutter. Following behind, you are often so busy cleaning up that you despair of finding time to be the kind of mother you think you should be.

At the end of the day, do you ever wonder what it's all about? By then, you may be too exhausted to dream.

It's easy to get discouraged as a parent. There's so much work and so little recognition. No one gives you a report card or performance review.

That's why you need to notice and hang on to the little things—the fact that your five-year-old has finally stopped whining, that your preadolescent son cleans the kitchen after dinner without being asked, that your eight-year-old actually does his homework without finagling, that your two-year-old has learned to hug the baby without smashing his nose.

With eleven children, I know I have better odds than most of finding a little progress in someone's life each day: something that gives me hope; something that helps me remember why I had them; something that makes it easier to wake up the next day with a smile. But I started out like all young mothers, with lots of work and little reward, learning how to live with toddlers.

Remember that parenting is one skill that can be learned only on the job. The biggest problem is that sometimes when we learn something new, it becomes a source of discouragement as we start to measure ourselves against an impossible standard. Be on guard against this as you go through parenthood; if you resist being too hard on yourself, you will never lose the joy of learning new things.

Begin by saying: "I will never be the perfect parent or the perfect teacher." Confidence is one of the greatest assets a parent can have. But note: Confidence does not mean that we do the job perfectly but that we have faith and are willing to do it to the best of our ability.

To this end, it is helpful to have an ideal to strive for. That way we can humbly examine ourselves to see where we might improve.

Yet, we should never allow high standards to become sources of bitterness or discouragement when we don't measure up to them. Let your ideals lift you up, not bring you down.

To put things in perspective, remember where your children came from; that is, remember though a mother's body bore them (yours or another's), they were entrusted to you specifically by God. This makes me believe that each of us is the perfect parent for our particular children—because God has perfectly matched us. And because God has different life plans for each child, He needs a wide variety of parents to raise them. That's why it's so important not to compare yourself with others or to become a slave to one particular method or ideology. Instead, gather information, then sift it through biblical truth, and look to God for all the final answers. He has given us an important mission, and we can count on Him to guide us through.

Do you know God loves you? Never lose sight of His love and forgiveness. He is not a critical parent, waiting to pounce on you at the first mistake you make. I am certain it is His desire that we feel confident enough in His love to model it for our children through the way we parent them. "So do not throw away your confidence; it will be greatly rewarded" (Heb. 10:35).

Even the best runners cannot win the race if they are doubtful and discouraged. I believe God wants us to be confident because we are then at our best. Our confidence is not found in ourselves or our methods but solely in Him.

If you have approached the task of raising children with a humble and open heart, if you are willing to grow and to change, if you are teachable, if you are ready to rely on God, then you are at the start line and ready to run the race.

Confidence does not mean that we do the job perfectly, but that we have faith and are willing to do it to the best of our ability.

Part Two
Get Set!

Five Potentials for Lifelong Learning

You're on your mark. Conditioning takes some stretching, but once you've stretched you're in a lot better shape to run the race. What do athletes say? "No pain, no gain."

With a few insights into yourself, some shifts in attitude here and there, the course is easier. You're already finding your toddlers easier to live with. They may feel the same way about you.

Don't forget to have a lot of fun. Blow bubbles. Take walks together and collect leaves. Lie on the grass and look at the clouds with your children. When it rains, run outside and get wet with them. Though God is doing a lot of serious work in our children during the toddler years, He also wants them to jump and giggle and be surprised. If you think of something spontaneous and unexpected, don't put it off. Do it.

We did it last summer. During the first week of August, our thermometers were setting records, with daily readings over 105 degrees. Because the Bay Area's climate is mild, we are ill-prepared to deal with prolonged bouts of heat. Air conditioning is rare, and fans are few and far between.

Four days of heavy heat and listless children were about all I could handle. On the fifth day I woke with a plan. By nine o'clock our van was loaded with car seats, kids, and coolers. We were off to the local rental store, where we rented a snow cone machine and loaded up on special cone-shaped cups, flavorings, and mountains of ice.

We came home and tried out the machine ourselves. It worked! After a round of snow cones, we all felt about twenty degrees cooler! And so we took that machine all over town: to job sites where my husband's employees were valiantly trimming trees, to Pop Warner football practice, to Special Ed classes. Back home again we invited all the neighborhood kids to cool off with us. For three days, we made snow cones from sunrise to sunset. I don't think my kids will ever forget it.

Before the great snow cone adventure, I didn't know I had something like that in me. No doubt about it, parenthood has helped me to become a more spontaneous person. Our children can bring out the best in us, if we let them.

Now how can we bring out the best in them?

In the following chapters, I will be answering some important questions about our children: What are the children's God-given potentials? How can we help them be released? How can we make the most of the toddler years so that our children will become all they are meant to be? And how can we prepare the children's heart to learn?

Created to Learn

Actually, a child's heart is already prepared to learn: God made it that way. A toddler is a bundle of relentless curiosity, investigating anything and everything he meets on his wobbly way. If you have begun more serious observation of your child, you have probably been amazed and delighted to see the thoroughness with which he examines his own small world.

Maria Montessori's interest in children was originally sparked when she observed children in the slums of Italy—children who had no toys and little stimulation—examining tiny crumbs on the floor of the tenements in which they lived. Their drive to explore and investigate despite their limited environment seemed close to miraculous.

I have observed my own children examining the tiniest leaves, pebbles, insect wings, holes in a lace-edged tablecloth. They bring an intensity with them in the way they relate to their world. God made them this way for a reason.

The toddler's curiosity is the catalyst that propels him into new ideas. Think of what it means in the life of a child the first time he drags a chair across the room to find out what's on those oh-so-high shelves. A toddler's life is crammed with learning breakthroughs, and this is just one: He has recognized that he has control of the environment (at least as long as no one takes it away!) and can manipulate it to attain what he wants.

All over the world toddlers follow the same pattern of development, experiencing learning breakthroughs independent of the adults around them. As long as the environment is not unusually deprived, the child will attain certain developmental milestones following a more or less common timetable.

In our homes, it can look so normal and everyday. But when you think about it, how extraordinary!

This has really come home to me since the birth of my son Jonathan, who has Down's syndrome.[1] Tripp and I were not disappointed to receive this little boy; we felt that God had a purpose in placing him in our family. We instinctively knew that through Jonathan God would teach us many lessons.

At first, I didn't know about Down's syndrome; so I began to research, to learn how I could help release Jonathan's God-given potentials.

What I discovered gave new meaning to what I had already learned about children. Remember what I said earlier about toddlers experiencing learning breakthroughs independent of the adults around them? This is not so true in the case of children with Down's syndrome. They require more help—called "early intervention"—to keep them on a reasonable schedule for gaining mastery of their environment. Without extra stimulation and encouragement, a Down's syndrome child might not walk before the age of five. With early intervention, the delay is considerably reduced. Average among his peers, Jonathan learned to walk at two-and-a-half. But it took a lot of love and energy from all in the family.

See why raising Jonathan—and now Jesse and Daniel, two babies with Down's syndrome we recently adopted—has given me a new appreciation for the drive to learn what God has built into most children? Living with Down's syndrome children is a blessing and a privilege. (Dale Evans wrote a book called *Angel Unaware* about her own Down's syndrome daughter.) But once you raise a child who requires a little extra, you realize how effortlessly most children come by the things they know.

A Toddler's Learning Process

Observing

It all begins with observation.

Once a toddler decides he needs an up-close look at something, no energy is spared. Christmas gifts require immediate unwrapping, fireplaces call for investigation, potted plants beg for uprooting to see what goes on underground. If you have a stool in your kitchen, you will find your toddler lugging it all over the room, hanging out at the counter to watch you at work and learning as he watches. Like the baby who is mentally grasping an object before his hand can quite get there, a toddler has learned "how" to talk on the phone before he even knows how to say words!

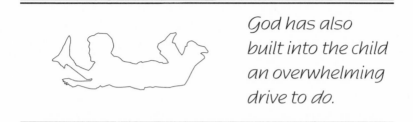

God has also built into the child an overwhelming drive to do.

No one needs to tell a child to observe or to investigate; he does it because God built into him a drive to learn about the world He created.[2] From infancy, before he can even reach for things, a baby is completely absorbed in the task of assimilating his environment visually—of using his eyes to make it his own.

Doing

Observation is, then, the first step in the learning process. But God has also built into the child an overwhelming drive to *do*. The child's observation becomes a catalyst for acquiring motor skills. He reaches for the rattle first with his eyes, then with hands. He notices some shiny keys a few feet away and scoots himself forward to capture them. He watches you peel carrots, and then he wants to do it himself.

When my Benjamin, as a toddler, discovered the dishwasher, he was fascinated by the connection between the sound of whooshing water and the switch. It didn't take him long to figure out how to start and stop the sound himself.

From then on, no dishwashing cycle remained uninterrupted. The instant Ben heard the swoosh of the water, he'd toddle, full of purpose, from wherever he was to pull that switch from right to left. Then, with a look of satisfaction, he'd toddle away, only to return the instant the machine was turned on again. He was a Man with a Mission! We so enjoyed his sense of accomplishment and good-natured acceptance of the machine that wouldn't stay still, that it often took hours to get the dishes done!

Doing is the second phase in the learning process. The child sees, then he does. And as each motor skill is acquired, it is immediately put to use mastering the environment.

It is in this second phase that things get tough for the adults in their lives. Because as surely as toddlers are driven to do, we seem driven to stop them.

And so the toddler years come to be known, ungraciously and unfairly, as the "terrible twos." We fret and complain at their lack of compliance, at the messes they make, the disorder they cause. We find ourselves saying, "No, no, no, no, no," like some warped and broken record. We spend a large part of these years at odds with our children.

I'm here to tell you things don't have to be this way. It is possible to thoroughly enjoy your children's toddler years! Give me the next few chapters, and I'll have you seeing your child differently. And as your understanding grows, your relationship will blossom.

Learning to Enjoy Your Toddler

Acceptance

First, we have to accept the doing—the toddler's drive to translate eyes-on to hands-on. Not that we allow our children to run wild or get themselves in trouble; but that we try to lovingly understand what motivates their actions.

Doing is the toddler's mission. This is how God made him. It is in fulfilling his specific mission that a toddler finds his greatest satisfaction. He gains confidence as he learns to master his environment. He continues being drawn to the next developmental challenge. Before you know it, he wants to tie his shoes, answer the phone, and feed the cat.

He also wants to investigate how much water the bathtub will hold (what's an overflow, anyway?), see how much toothpaste is in the tube, and find out whether the baby will scream if he sits on him.

The following chapters will equip you to "read" your child's motivations and respond to them appropriately. You will discover ways to meet your child's needs so adequately that they will not find expression in negative ways.

Remember, I live with my research. What I have to share is still being tested each day in my own home with my own children: six-month-old Daniel, eighteen-month-old Jesse, three-year-old Madeleine, and four-year-old Jonathan (developmentally more like two-and-a-half). I am also seeing the long-range results in Sophia (7), Zachary (8), Benjamin (10), Matthew (12), Joshua (13), Jasmine (21), and Samantha (27).

Our toddlers are like little packages of promise, just waiting to be unwrapped. My aim is to help you discover how to release your children's God-given potentials for learning, so that they might become all that they can become. And so that you will enjoy the process.

Recognizing Sensitive Periods

It seems that with the drives to observe, to do, to master the environment, God has also built into each child certain potentials that will enable him to continue loving to learn. I identify these potentials as independence, order, self-control, concentration, and service.

Each of these potentials has its sensitive period during the toddler years. This is a limited time when—if the conditions are right—the potential will become firmly rooted as part of the child's character. By right conditions, I mean appropriate environmental cues, plus loving parents or teachers who understand the child's drives and try to steer his course in the right direction.

This is not to say that a child whose sensitive period for order is missed will forever remain disorganized. But theory has it—and my experience concurs—that once the sensitive period has passed, only by a major act of the will can an older child or adult develop a character quality that could have come easily and gracefully in the toddler years. Worse yet, when the sensitive period is discouraged, or even trampled upon, we often see unhealthy, unproductive, and antisocial patterns in later years.

God has also built into each child certain potentials that will enable him to continue loving to learn . . . independence, order, self-control, concentration, and service.

Sensitive periods could be referred to in today's language as windows of opportunity. That's a good word picture. When the window is open, you can be part of the action; when it's closed, it's hard for you to be a major part of what's going on inside. The window is open only for a few years; they are limited periods of time—well before kindergarten—when we have access to the foundation of our child's character in a way that no one will ever have again.

The following chapters will help you understand the sensitive periods for independence, order, self-control, concentration, and service—and equip you to effectively release these God-given potentials in your child.

I have found through my workshops that once parents understand the importance of sensitive periods in the child's life, they become more patient around, more responsive to, and more satisfied with their toddlers.

But there's more—their toddlers become more patient, responsive, and satisfied as well! If that's almost enough to keep you reading in between the runny noses and the loads of laundry, I hope it helps to know we're in this together! After all, I'm writing to you in between the same chores!

Five Potentials for Joyful Lifelong Learning

Toddler Potential	Ready Signals	Reinforcement	Short-Term Benefit	Long-Term Benefit
INDEPENDENCE "I can do it!"	❧ Seeking self-reliance ❧ Frustration	❧ Make doing possible ❧ Extra time ❧ Extra care ❧ Different approach	Satisfaction	Confidence
ORDER "Where does it (where do I) belong?"	❧ Stacking objects ❧ Closing doors and drawers	❧ Child-friendly environment ❧ A place for everything ❧ Sequencing	Security	Efficiency

SELF CONTROL "What are my limits?"	❧ Imitating adults, e.g., at prayer
	❧ Ability to hold still for short periods
		❧ Gross motor challenges:
		  Walking on line
		  Walking with bell
		❧ Tuning into silence
		❧ Small Beginnings exercise
			Peace	Well-being

CONCENTRATION "Quiet! Mind at work!"	❧ Examining small objects ❧ Absorption in any specific activity	❧ Observe what clicks ❧ Invite repetition	Ability to learn	Productivity
SERVICE "Let me help!"	❧ Desire to participate in household chores	❧ Share housework ❧ Accept results ❧ Encourage and praise	Self-worth	Meaningful life

Chapter Six

Independence: "I Can Do It!"

"No, lemme doowit myseff!"

Sound familiar? It's the rallying cry of toddlers every-where. At this moment, throughout the world—in hun-dreds of languages—children are telling their parents they want to do it themselves.

- 🐦 In Taiwan, Li Na is struggling with the buttons on her blouse, resisting her mother's efforts to take over and do it faster.

- 🐦 In Luxembourg, Jorgen's eyes fill with tears as his mother takes the pitcher from his hand—he wants to pour his own milk, sweet and fresh from the cow.

- 🐦 By the river in a remote African village, Kamaria push-es away two hands offering too much help and contin-ues her efforts to balance the basket of fish on her head—just the way her mother does.

- 🐦 In Tokyo, Akira strains on tiptoe to unhook the latch of the gate, then sobs in frustration because his fa-ther's more capable hand reaches first and does it for him.

🍎 In Nebraska, Joseph collapses on the floor and wails when his big brother, with enviably longer legs, answers the door before he can get there himself.

"No, I dooit!" The words are simple, direct, and from the heart. They are also among the most frustrating we adults ever hear. Even worse are the wails and whines, clenched fists, squinched faces, flailing limbs, and melodramatic falls our toddlers use to tell us how much they resent our doing things for them.

When these push our buttons, we may find ourselves wailing and clenching too—well, maybe more on the inside than out. We may be more self-controlled; still, there's no question that these toddler tactics cause us to react—usually by digging in our heels and making things worse.

In childhood development there is a universal language of independence. We are on the other side of the struggle, but we would do well to remember where we started. Because, as a matter of fact, everyone's march to maturity begins under the same banner.

In the beginning, each of us wanted to do it all ourselves.

How to Meet Your Child's Need for Independence

See It Their Way

Maybe we should start by seeing it the way they see it: You want to put on your own socks. Your hands are small but your determination is great. Your concentration is broken when along comes someone big, someone who can put them on better and faster, someone who wants to do it for you. After all, everyone's running late. You don't know exactly what late means other than your mother is about to lose her temper. But there are these socks—you can't think about anything else. Your existence has become focused on one need. You are compelled, pushed, driven to put these socks on your very own feet.

But these big hands are pushing your little hands aside and pulling the socks away. These big hands that are usually filled with love and understanding now offer only opposition. What recourse is there but to fight?

What life struggle would give you, as an adult, the where-withal to engage in hand-to-hand combat against an opponent packing five hundred pounds on a twelve-foot frame? Can you even imagine such odds?

How spectacular it is that we privileged to live with the waist-high-and-under actually witness such displays of courage in our own homes each day! And all over little things like shoes and socks, buttons and barrettes, pitchers and sugar bowls.

Why do they do it? What could possibly give them the determination, the tenacity, the foolhardiness to persist in the struggle?

Look at the Big Picture

Some might call what we've described "rebelliousness" or "intractability." Then the explanation would be easy. Blame it on the fall—when Adam and Eve deliberately disobeyed God's command.

But twenty-five years of studying, teaching, and living with children have shown me that the answer is not quite so simple. Yes, each of us is flawed from birth, and even children need the Lord.[1] Still, original sin does not cover all the territory in the daily struggles of a three-year-old.

Instead, I believe that the intensity with which children pursue "doing it themselves" demonstrates that the drive for independence is a God-given potential—a potential for good. Rather than the fall of man, it may even represent his glory.

A radical statement like that requires an explanation, I know. Let me give it a try.

The major problem with children's drive for independence is that it occurs when the effects of the fall are running rampant in their little personalities. Since the drive for independence begins around two years, not many children experience the beginning of this sensitive period while being in a tractable, teachable mode. That is why, mixed in with this very valuable potential for good, there is a lot of negative behavior.

But there is a difference between trying to pour your own cereal and making your mother chase you all around the grocery store and through the parking lot. The first is an example of wanting to take care of your needs, and the second is an act of rebellion.

Discipline When Necessary

Many of our parenting problems stem from lumping both types of behavior together, then reacting to either the same way. If this has been the case for you, try a fresh approach. When you feel impatient with your child, take a deep breath. Then, before reacting, ask yourself if the child's behavior is rebellious and destructive or whether it is the natural result of his drive for independence.

If the behavior is rebellious or destructive, then it should be handled as a discipline problem. Here I must acknowledge that while there is some overlap in the area of learning development and child discipline, the scope of this book is limited to the former. In the area of child discipline, I lean on the experts. In appendix A, you will find resources for Christian parents containing a wealth of trustworthy information on sensible, effective child discipline.

I've chosen the best from the sky-high stack of books I've accumulated in twenty-seven years of teaching and parenting. Frankly, if there were never another book written on child discipline, we'd all be in great shape simply by following the advice of compassionate, caring Christian professionals like Dr. James Dobson and Dr. William Sears.

Any discipline problems in our own home (yes, we have a few!) are not due to a lack of available, comprehensive information, nor even a lack of time to read. I must confess that when we get off course, it's not because we don't know better. Instead, it's due to a lack of consistent application of what my husband and I already know will work.

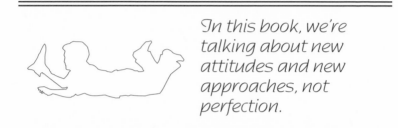

In this book, we're talking about new attitudes and new approaches, not perfection.

So my admittedly simple message about discipline is this: Read the experts and follow their advice as faithfully as you can, giving yourself a little room to be sometimes too busy, too distracted, or too tired to be the perfect parent.

Take Heart

When you start thinking Small Beginnings, you begin to see things a little differently. You may be anxious to get rid of some old patterns and try a more positive, productive approach. But in developing new habits, you will find yourself occasionally reverting to the old.

I do it too!

Don't be disappointed or discouraged. In this book, we're talking about new attitudes and new approaches, not perfection.

The ability to discern between rebellion and the drive for independence is key for Small Beginnings. As parents, we need this as our starting point, because actually we will be doing two things at once: setting boundaries to curb rebellious behavior, while encouraging our child's drive for independence in a positive direction.

Our role as parents is demanding, calling for close attention and play-by-play decisions (reminding me a little of a football referee). Does this stamping of the foot signal rebellion, or does it mean I need to take a second look at the situation to see if it's an "I doit myself" issue?

Sharpen Your Focus

Right now, you may be wondering why it is so important to encourage the drive for independence at such an early age. Can't it be put off until later? The answer is emphatically no.

Remember our discussion of sensitive periods? Think about the sensitive period for language, which begins very obviously around two years of age. In order for language to develop properly in the child, he must have opportunities to hear language spoken and speak it himself. Children from language-rich environments have wide vocabularies and are comfortable with their language, while children raised in deprivation have limited language skills and struggle to improve them later.

Perhaps not quite so obvious, but just as strong, the sensitive period for independence begins shortly after the second birthday. When you know which clues to watch for, the period will become very apparent. You will begin to differentiate clearly between rebellion and independence.

You will find, as you learn to discern, that the child begins his drive for independence by focusing on self-reliance skills. He wants to do things for himself, like taking off and putting on his own clothes—sometimes many times a day. He is always looking for a new challenge, like getting into and out of his own car seat or cracking the eggs open for breakfast.

These are good things, things you want to encourage, even if it means constantly refolding clothes and putting them away. Even if it means a few elusive eggshells in the scrambled eggs. Later I will share ways in which you can help children accomplish the things that you may feel uneasy about letting them try.

Think Ahead

First I want to get you excited about your child's developing self-reliance, give you a glimpse of the future, and share with you the benefits of raising a child whose independence needs have been met at the proper time.[2]

While the sensitive period for independence unfolds in the same way as the sensitive period for language, the effects of enrichment or deprivation are perhaps even more long-ranging. A child who is not given opportunities in this area at this special time will be a child who struggles later on with independence issues. He may remain dependent on others to direct him through life. At the other extreme, he may eventually become the rebellious teenager, driven to assert his delayed independence in antisocial ways.

By contrast, the toddler whose parents have paved the path to healthy independence will have what it takes to become a self-reliant child. He will enjoy the satisfaction of doing things for himself. He will not be the one helplessly whining about the location of his shoes each morning, nor the one who needs supervision to get his homework done each night.

Independence is an essential building block of character, one whose presence or absence becomes very apparent during the teen years. A child whose independence needs were met at the right time in the right spirit—with appropriate boundaries being set—will grow into a teen you can count on. That teen will have a true independent spirit, with no axes to grind and an ability to make decisions based on his own values rather than going along with his peers.

An independent teenager will want to work, will look forward to the day when he can take care of himself, is not afraid of the future. You will never find him looking for a handout.

Looking into adulthood, independence is a must-have for anyone called upon to lead or follow with wisdom. While as Christians we are dependent on our Heavenly Father and the guidance of the Holy Spirit, each of us needs the strength of character to think independently, to be able to examine information to determine if it matches the truth. Healthy independence, coupled with godly values, enables an individual to go against the flow—that is, to do what's right when everyone else is doing what's wrong.

Understanding the role of independence, the benefits to the individual and our society, may help you to take a different approach to what people ungraciously call "the terrible twos." Taking the long view helps you in those frustrating moments when you are cleaning up spilled milk after your future model citizen!

How to Foster Independence

They want to do things themselves. We've decided to let them. How do we do it?

Be Observant

One night a few years ago I turned on the water for fifteen-month-old Madeleine's bath and, as part of the well-worn routine, turned to scoop her toys from the basket to the tub. But there she was behind me, bending, picking out one toy at a time, throwing each delightedly into the water.

Beaming broadly, full of toddler confidence, she radiated without words, "I'll take over from here, Mom."

I got the message loud and clear.

When your child surprises you by taking a small step toward independence, your hugs and smiles show her you care. Even better is when you stay a step ahead.

Use your observation skills to notice when your child is ready to try something new. For instance, if I had been observing closely, if I had been thinking Small Beginnings, I might have realized that Madeleine could put her own toys in the tub and invited her weeks before to "do it herself." Then she'd have the double delight of a step toward self-reliance and a mommy who was anticipating her next skill.

Provide Opportunities

Be constantly on the lookout for the next step your child can take in "doing it himself." By providing opportunities for your child to grow in independence, you will meet this need in positive and safe ways, thereby eliminating showdowns over things that don't matter.

What happens when your child's next step toward independence is not such an easy one to handle? For instance, what do you do when you come into the kitchen and find your three-year-old on the verge of pouring a glass of iced tea? (a) scream, (b) break out in a cold sweat, (c) act nonchalant so he won't get scared and drop the pitcher, then artfully take it away, (d) say a quick prayer, smile encouragingly, and say something like, "Oh, are you going to pour your own? May I help you?"

Be alert to opportunities to stretch yourself in this area. Take a chance (when it's safe to do so) and let your toddler meet the challenges he sets for himself. Relax and realize that spilled iced tea is not really such a big deal.

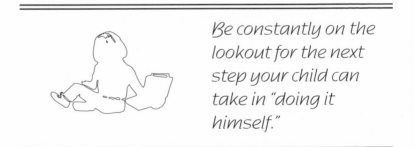

Be constantly on the lookout for the next step your child can take in "doing it himself."

Look at it this way: If you woke up tomorrow with a burning desire to water ski, your friends would never squelch you by saying you weren't ready. Nor would they wait for signs of your becoming ready. Instead, they would offer instruction and pointers to maximize your chances of success. Before your interest wore thin, they would get you up on the skis. If you fell down, they wouldn't take away your water skis and complain what a mess you'd made. Instead, they'd minimize your clumsiness, encouraging you to try again. That's how grown-ups treat each other when one of us wants to learn something new.

Think of this the next time your child thinks he's ready to do something—like pouring his own milk—and you think he isn't. Sometimes the only reason he's not ready is that he's never had an opportunity to try.

Keep in mind that, just like us, children want to succeed. Sometimes it's helpful to point out the pitfalls: "Try using your other hand to hold the pitcher underneath. . . . Aim for the middle of the glass. . . . Don't forget to stop when the glass is full!" However, nothing is accomplished when we rush to take over—nothing except the reminder that we are the ones who know it all and can do it all.

Granted, there are many things young children cannot and should not do by themselves. And when the child's actions place him in danger, a parent must emphatically say no, acting swiftly to keep the child safe. Aside from those situations, though, there are many things children can safely do for themselves.

Unfortunately, when we are on automatic pilot, we often say no when we could say yes. Encourage your child's independence by looking for ways to make things possible for him.

Take extra time. Making things possible may be as simple as slowing down a little. Being a parent of toddlers means you almost always were supposed to be somewhere five minutes ago. Because of the hurry in our own lives, we often find ourselves putting a shirt on someone who really could have done it himself.

Make it a point to give your child the time he needs to do things for himself. When you are going out, plan an extra fifteen minutes to get ready. Give your child the time he needs to get himself ready in whatever ways he has mastered. Let him know you're counting on him. This kind of time invested in your child costs nothing, but will pay off in big dividends later on.

Take extra care. Often there are little things we can turn over to our toddlers if we just teach them a little extra care. Would you be surprised if I told you that your two-year-old can be taught to carry a cereal bowl to the table without spilling? All it takes is him seeing you do it first. Your thoughtful and careful modeling will make possible for him a small accomplishment that will bring him enormous satisfaction.

Demonstrate by using two hands, watching the bowl as you walk, and walking slowly and carefully. Exaggerate! If you slow down and concentrate, your child will be mesmerized, I promise. Show how to set the bowl on the table before sitting down. Show concern about it being far enough from the edge not to fall off. Now let him try. Remember not to fill the bowl too full!

Often there are little things we can turn over to our toddlers if we just teach them a little extra care.

Children are born imitators. The best way to avoid spills and messes is not by keeping everything out of their hands, but by using exaggerated care in the little things they watch us do, then giving them opportunities to join.

Try this Small Beginnings method for a week—modeling extra care and challenging your child by turning over new responsibilities. You'll be surprised at how your little ones will rise to the challenge. Just remember, if they're brave enough to fight giants, they may be valiant enough to make it across the kitchen without spilling!

Use a fresh approach. Sometimes a task can be too challenging for a child to conquer even with extra time and extra care. Here we need to rethink a task to find a fresh approach.

Take, for instance, putting on a coat. When I taught preschoolers, I could have spent our entire recess just putting twenty-five jackets on twenty-five wiggling bodies, just in time to take them off and come back to class. How grateful I was to learn that two-year-olds can jacket themselves!

Here's how: Show your child how to lay his jacket on the floor in front of him, open wide. The neck should be closest to him, the bottom of the jacket farthest away. In this position, even the youngest child can be taught to bend, put his arms in the sleeves, and flip the jacket overhead. The sleeves slide down the arms to the shoulders, and a satisfied toddler needs only to be zipped.

Only a few seconds saved? Yes. Could this really be that important to a mom with fewer than twenty-five children to jacket? Yes, more important than meets the eye.

Because much more than saving seconds is going on here. Think of it as part of a pattern—a pattern of looking for ways to answer your child's independence needs, a pattern of turning bits and pieces of responsibility over to him as he grows.

Encourage Your Child

Always encourage your child's efforts, even when the results are less than perfect. A child learning to dress himself doesn't care so much if his shirt is inside-out. Wait until he's enjoyed putting on his own shirt a few times before gently instructing him, "Oh, look at these buttons! Did you know that shirts have an inside and outside? How can we fix it?"

Of course, we want to spur the child to do his best, but use discretion. The first time a child accomplishes some task on his own is not the time to lower the boom. In encouraging him to improve, treat him with the same kindness and consideration you would a friend.

Beyond the toddler years, continue to look for ways to encourage your child's independence. As soon as he can tell time, buy him a clock and let him wake up to his own alarm and morning routine. Teach him to make his own breakfast or lunch.

Again, it's worth emphasizing that the time you devote to helping your child become independent is an important investment in the future. If your child is given encouragement to "do it himself" during the sensitive period for independence, he will grow to be competent and confident.

An old maxim says, "Give a man a fish, and he will eat for a day; show him how to fish, and he will eat forever." As a parent, I have found the greatest satisfaction watching my children's self-reliance grow as they depend on me not to do things for them but to teach them how to do things for themselves.

When you need a little extra patience to allow him to "do it himself," remember that because of your encouragement in the early years, your child will never be the one helplessly waiting for Mom to complete his seventh-grade science project!

Think of it this way: Parenting is one job we should be working ourselves out of each day!

I can do everything through him who gives me strength.
Philippians 4:13

Chapter Seven

Order: "Where Does It (Where Do I) Belong?"

No one needs convincing that the toddler years are when the drive for independence is strongest. But would it surprise you to learn that the sensitive period for order is strongest at that time as well?

Moms and dads who spend their days bending, scooping up blocks, blankets, and baby dolls may be quick to disagree. And I admit, because I'm still scooping up after four myself, it often takes a mighty stretch of my own imagination to remember that the seeds of order exist in those busy bodies.

Seeds. That is the best word to describe how the potential for order is built into children. If we think of independence as a wild vine growing nonstop in all directions—a vine that takes careful tending, pruning, and guidance to help it produce the best fruit—then yes, order is dramatically different. Independence is more like a tiny seed waiting for the right soil to allow it to flourish.

This chapter will equip you to provide the best growing ground for the seed God has planted in each child—the potential for order.

Sowing Seeds of Order

But first, we'll take the long view. The nursery man couldn't convince you to choose a seed packet and put special care into its contents without a picture of the fruit on the front. Likewise, parents need a vision of the potential in their children. If you are impressed by the fruit that will result, you will be more willing to put in the extra planning and labor it might take to produce it.

The drive to independence produces noteworthy fruit. In the last chapter, we looked at the big picture to see the results we could expect from encouraging our child's independence needs in appropriate ways. We saw that leadership and discernment—the ability to do what's right rather than what's easy or popular—depends on this healthy foundation.

The potential for order is of a different character. It produces something more like ground cover. At maturity, it doesn't attract much notice, but provides a beautiful background for the rest of the garden. And when a slope is threatening to slide, it even holds the soil together to keep the hill from crumbling.

Provides Stability

When times are tough, when storms are knocking down the more conspicuous greenery, order not only brings comfort, but that may be all that holds each day together until the storm has passed.

The most visible order in my life has to do with laundry. With eleven children and their hundreds of pursuits, we can accumulate a mountain chain of laundry in less than three days. Never having had an interest in mountain climbing, I decided early that I would wash clothes every day. Moreover, since it is easier to do the things I have to do if I stop loathing and start loving, I made a decision years ago to love my laundry. I also learned to use that time to spend time with the Lord.

Now, because I've spent so many moments with Him there, my laundry room has become my prayer closet, my hiding place, my anchor. Each day may be different, but one thing's for sure: There is laundry. And no matter how pressed for time I am, I can sing and pray while the clothes get clean.

When my son Jonathan was born four years ago, he had many medical problems. It was one of the most difficult periods of my life, with seven children at home and a tiny baby in a big university hospital. Trying to be there for everyone, I would wait for my husband each evening to take over at the hospital, then drive home, barely coping with the emotion and exhaustion.

Staggering in the front door, my steps became more purposeful as I made a beeline for my laundry room, too tired even to pray. Only when I had sorted the laundry, unrolled the balled-up socks, measured the soap, and heard the whoosh of the water could I relax and spend time with the children.

A superficial observer might have questioned my sanity. But no one would have questioned that I always walked out of my laundry room a little refreshed.

Now I see that as my world seemed to be falling apart, and our family structure was so out of whack, I was holding on by a thin thread of laundry. It was the one event I could count on, the tangible thing that was always the same. It represented peace, stability, and order.

Created by God

Order is not an easy subject for some adults. Many of us struggle with order ourselves, or at least some aspects of it. Some are disorganized, forgetful, or habitually late. We're "set in our ways," and so we are resigned to our bad habits, maybe even defensive of them.

But how does God see it? I have often thought of God's act of creation and how He created the world with order, accomplishing one specific task each day and finally resting when everything was complete.

I thought of creation itself, how order is built into it, making life possible. The earth revolves at a precise distance around the sun, for example. Any nearer or farther and we would burn or freeze to death. The tilt of the earth's axis makes the seasons possible, year after year. The speed of rotation is consistent, giving a regularity to our waking and sleeping. Gravity holds it all together. All was created with precision and a high regard for order.

If we're committed to giving our best to our children, we need to appreciate God's potential for order. We need to ask how He might like to see things done. My own view is this: Just as the orderly precision of the universe keeps it running smoothly, order on the human level makes for ease of living.

Webster's New World Dictionary has twenty meanings for *order*. The second definition is "a state of peace and serenity." Is it only coincidence that the next two definitions are "the sequence or arrangements of things or events" and "a fixed or definite plan, system, arrangement"?

No, not a coincidence, according to my experience. I am certain that we find peace and serenity in environments that are planned and arranged with an eye to order.

How to Aim for Order

Make a Decision

As I said before, order—though a God-given potential in each child—is not of the same character as independence. The child's need for order is not so powerful. You don't find yourself butting heads with it, seeking to stifle it, coming to grips with it.

The potential for order lies in wait like a dormant seed within the child. You will see signs of it only when planted in the right soil—soil that has been properly prepared to encourage its growth. Once the seed has sprouted, you will need to give it a lot of attention and care to keep it alive and well. It may not be the fastest growing plant, but once established it will surprise you with how little maintenance it requires.

> *If parents provide the proper environment and encourage the child's potential, if they are patient and persistent, they will see wonderful results: a child with a strong sense of order— a foundation for peace and serenity.*

In more practical terms, if parents provide the proper environment and encourage the child's potential, if they are patient and persistent, they will see wonderful results: a child with a strong sense of order—a foundation for peace and serenity.

If order is not something that comes easily to you, but you understand the benefits to your child, remember you can change! Our children's character and future are worth any amount of effort to be the best we can be.

The first step is to make a decision. The second step is to aim for order in your own life and the running of the household. The third is to fit the environment as much as possible to meet the needs of the child.

See It Their Way

I am not suggesting that the world revolve around our children. But our homes are already equipped to meet the needs of adults. It might be interesting to spend a little time seeing them through our children's eyes.

I once saw a store display with a wooden chair that was almost eight feet tall. The seat came up to my chest, and if I stood beside it and looked up, the back seemed to rise above me forever. I had the strangest feeling of inadequacy standing next to it. If someone had asked me to take a seat, I would have felt ridiculous.

Then I thought what it would be like to live in a world where everything was so out of proportion to me. Where I had to stand on tiptoe and swipe my hand blindly across the surface of a shelf to find out what was up there—only to get in trouble for spilling or breaking something. Where someone took my jacket and hung it up for me when it would be so nice to be able to reach a place to hang it myself. Where all the excitement seemed to be happening on the kitchen counter, too remote for me to see.

No wonder God built them with a compulsion to climb! Otherwise they'd collapse from frustration or boredom.

Have you ever wondered what it felt like to sit at the kitchen table to color, feet dangling helplessly from a booster seat?

And what about these toy baskets? If a child could speak, he might say something like this: "I can't find anything in these heaps of toys, and so I dump them all out; but that seems to make everyone pretty unhappy, especially when it turns out there wasn't anything there I wanted to do anyway. What are they there for?

"I want to know what you're making for breakfast. I want to know where everything is. And why are all the pictures hung where I can't see them? You're always too busy to look at them, but I would."

Create a Child-Friendly Space

A child can't tell us these things. And by the time we grow up, we've forgotten how desperately small and inconsequential we felt in relation to the world we lived in. One reason young children love going to preschool is because there they finally enter a world where their needs are met.

Our homes cannot, of course, revolve completely around children; they need to meet our needs as well. But there are many adaptations we can make to better meet children's needs without neglecting our own.

A child-friendly space is related to order, as you will see. But it also meets independence needs and security needs. Think of how much freedom and security we have in an environment scaled to our needs. Then think how little our children have.

Keep in mind in the suggestions that follow, many aspects of the child's developmental needs are woven together in creating a child-friendly space. As each item is discussed, think how it would work to make the child more self-reliant, secure, and self-confident.

Child-sized furniture. Start with the basics. This means a place to sit and work that fits and feels comfortable. A child-sized table and chair set is an investment you will never regret. Your toddler is sure to be delighted by furniture tailored to his proportions.

For endurance, wood is best—I have had mine through eight children. If new furniture is beyond your budget, check garage sales and second-hand stores to find it used. Once we know what our children need, God has a way of providing it at a cost we can afford. There are also sturdy plastic sets available at discount toy stores.

Once you bring the table and chairs home, do not put them in your child's bedroom. They will only collect dust. Think of it this way: Would we use tables in our own bedrooms? Maybe that's why we don't put them there.

Instead, put the table and chairs where the life of the family is centered—some place where he can do things and still be very much a part of the hustle and bustle of daily life. Not only will he use it often, but you will have the satisfaction of seeing your child at work.

A special workplace. Even if you are short of space, look for just a corner that can be a special work area for your child. You may have to come to grips with some preconceived ideas about home decorating, but the sooner we drop our aspirations to have a designer house the happier everyone in the home will be. Besides, we can all be perfectionists later to keep ourselves busy and take our minds off Empty Nest Syndrome.

Finding a spot for your child to work comfortably, without being separated from the rest of the family, is top priority in the preschool years. Sooner than you can imagine, privacy will become a priority for your child. Then you will wish he wasn't always disappearing into his bedroom.

Kitchen companion. Another way to enjoy more companionship with your child is by bringing him up to your level in the kitchen. A stool next to the counter will open a whole new world to him as he watches you sift, measure, mix, and pour.

If you are concerned about safety when you're not around, stash the stool in a closet. Just don't get too in a hurry to bother getting it out. Try not to miss these precious moments when you and your child can see things almost eye-to-eye.

Child-friendly decorating. Think of your children as you decorate. Choose colors and upholstery that will please them as well as the adults in the house. At a garage sale recently, I found a love seat covered in a Grandma Moses type pattern—farmhouses, cows, chickens, and dogs. I snatched it up, not so much for me and my husband, but more because it made me smile to think how much my kids would love to look at it.

Beside the love seat, I set a display table with a heavy glass top and slide-out display drawer. But instead of putting anything impressive in it, I arranged my children's assortment of fast-food freebies.

Facing the love seat is a stand of children's books. It's not surprising that this whimsical oasis has become a favorite spot for a good read.

Even in the living room, our coffee table holds children's art books and magazines, rather than adult reading material. I can always think of where to find something to browse through, but my children need things up close and personal to make them interesting.

When I buy pictures, I choose ones that will be interesting to my children too. Children love classical art, perhaps because they will often spend enough time looking at the picture to get the whole story. The toddler years are the perfect time to begin to stimulate in your child a lifelong appreciation of art.

Don't forget to hang at least a few pictures (and a mirror or two) low enough for your children to enjoy. Greeting cards are so beautiful, and inexpensive frames so plentiful, you can create many miniature art works for next to nothing. Then think of yourself as three or four feet high, take a trip around your house, and find all the nooks and crannies where your children will be sure to notice them.

Even if you find this inspirational—in a fun kind of way—you may be wondering how this relates to order and to the child's ability to learn. Here is the connection: Our surroundings say something about us. That's why some of us spend even a little too much time decorating, and why your house looks different than your neighbor's. The environment also sends a message to children. Usually it tells them they are helpless and unimportant. If their personalities don't impact the environment, they could feel like they're just passing through, much the same as we feel in a hotel.

A child-friendly environment sends a much different message. The home is ordered in such a way as to take the needs of the child into account. This gives your child assurance that he is a vital, contributing member of the family. For instance, a stool in the kitchen tells your child not only that you trust him, but also that you welcome his company. A picture hung at his level tells him that you care.

Just as important, these things communicate something about the child's place in the world. They give him a sense of belonging, of "fitting in." In this way, a sense of order begins to be established in the child.

The best learning takes place in an environment that is comfortable and secure, built on a foundation of order.

The best learning takes place in an environment that is comfortable and secure, built on a foundation of order. Making our homes child-friendly is like adding nutrients to the soil to better nurture the seeds of order in our children.

Instill a Love of Order

But we need to dig deeper. Since our children are Little Mirrors, our own ability to keep order in the environment is essential. Here is where the soil may need more than nutrients—it may need a rototiller! If order is not your own strong point, it might help to think of how it would make your own life easier if it were.

One of my sons, now eleven, is a terrific guy in many respects: bright, cheerful, fun to be with. But he struggles greatly because of his lack of order. He loses time and patience when he can't find his shoes, his homework, or his football helmet.

At points like this, parents are prone to ask what went wrong. After all, this son had the same mother and father, the same home as his brothers and sisters.

The truth is, nothing "went wrong." Though the potentials exist in each child, each child is a unique blend of strengths and weaknesses. If we are providing all that we can to encourage the child's potentials, then we can be confident in the job we have done as parents. When they have problems later on, we can keep guiding them in the right direction, but we don't need to spend a lot of time feeling like we must have failed.

Even with the same seeds in the same soil, one plant can seem hardier than the one next to it. So you give the one next to it a little extra care. That's what I do with my disorderly son, who wishes to remain nameless in case his future wife ever reads this book. Now that we've gone beyond the sensitive period, I have to rely on my powers of persuasion to convince him of the advantages of order. Then I need to encourage him to use his will, to make a decision to choose order in his life.

The good news is that through an act of the will (backed by prayer), it is possible to bring about strength in a weak area.

If you could use more order in your life, it's never too late to change. It just takes more conscious effort.

But what a gift for your children!

Have a Place for Everything

A two-year-old needs an environment that makes sense to him. When he is surrounded by order and when it is brought to his attention, he will naturally want to contribute to it. Seize that window of opportunity by giving him many ways to keep things in order. Begin by having a place for everything and everything in its place.

Put a peg rack at his height near the front door so he can hang up his own jacket when he comes in. A boot tray underneath will keep dirt off your carpets and help him remember where his shoes are.

Keep things organized in an attractive way. Life with children means life with all kinds of assorted odds and ends, so toy boxes and baskets will always be with us—but make them a last resort.

Opt for shelves whenever you can. White shelves are best because toys and learning materials look most attractive on a white surface, and children will be drawn to them. I buy white laminate shelves 36" high and 9" deep that you assemble yourself. They are bright and easy to keep clean. Try to buy extra shelves (check for a store that has them available), so that one bookcase can hold a lot of organized stuff.

Start with a low bookcase next to your toddler's table. This is the place for the Small Beginnings exercises as well as puzzles and other learning materials your child can work with at the table.

Put as many shelves as you can afford near your toddler's table, in his room, or wherever you want your child to spend time. Use baskets or plastic containers (buy on sale when you can, or try garage sales) to sort and hold things like small blocks, beads and laces, pegs, whatever would otherwise be part of the jumbled mess in the toy box.

Now, teach your child to take out one thing at a time, to spend as much time as he wants with it, and then to put it back before taking out anything else.

If you have more than one child, you will want to teach the youngest that he can take from the shelves only what he has been shown how to use. This is imperative, as some of the Small Beginnings exercises are delicate. Believe it or not, it is also possible. As with all rules, you make them known clearly to the child and then consistently see that they are carried out.

A Lifelong Appreciation of Order

The order that you see in this plan is built into the Small Beginnings exercises you will learn later on. Order is also about pattern and sequence, and so we can reinforce the child's awareness of order by breaking down any activity into component steps, by talking things through from start to finish: "Should we make some carrot sticks? OK, first we get the carrots out of the refrigerator. Now we need to get the peeler. Now we peel the carrot. . . . The carrot's peeled, so now we can cut it into sticks. Now they're ready to eat!"

You see, that's how life really is, sequenced and orderly, one action following another. Order provides your child with a feeling of security. When he knows where to hang his jacket, where to put his shoes and toys, he feels less helpless and more competent.

Your own understanding of your child's needs in this area, and your loving provision will nurture the God-given potential in your child for order in his life and work. This will make it easier for him to accomplish all that he undertakes.

At the same time, as you begin making changes in your home to provide better soil for the seed, you will find yourself more sensitive to order and to its benefits for each of us. You may develop a deep appreciation for the order inherent in the world God gave us.

And in order, you may find a place of rest for your own spirit. Even when you are overwhelmed by many demands, with order as a ground cover—holding it all together—you may be surprised to find that

❧

The peace of God, which transcends all understanding,
will guard your hearts and your minds in Christ Jesus.
Philippians 4:7

Chapter Eight

Self-Control:
"What Are My Limits?"

A lot of primping and preparation had gone into this event before we even set foot in the elegant building. Now our family was finally here—at the San Francisco Symphony, eager for the annual Lollipop Concert to begin.

Included in our preparation had been not only learning about instruments and composers, but also sitting still and listening. I knew the children were ready to get the most out of this unique experience.

We had battled rush-hour traffic, seized a hard-to-come-by parking space (whispering a prayer of thanks), safely negotiated several crosswalks and numerous hustlers trying to share our money or their message, rummaged through Mom's purse to find the wayward tickets, made the obligatory bathroom rounds, and finally wound our way to our balcony seats.

As I sank into the rich plush velvet, I breathed a sigh of relief and gazed at the ceiling, a canopy tranquil as the clouds. I could have easily sat for days just soaking in the soothing colors and textures. The hectic few hours before began to melt away. If I had been thinking in words, they might have gone something like this: "What a gift God gives us to allow us the ability to rest—like throwing an exhausted swimmer a life preserver!"

The more settled I became though, the more in contrast I felt to the audience that was quickly assembling. At the curb, school bus after school bus was dropping classes from all over the Bay Area. As the clusters of twenty-five or thirty children began to fill the rows, the life preserver analogy took on a more ironic meaning.

On every side, above and below, was a vast and churning multicolored sea. A frothy, foamy ocean of tapping legs and jerking arms, twitching hands and feet, bouncing shoulders and bobbing heads.

Here and there, like dolphins breaking the surface, children popped spontaneously and completely out of their seats to grab a person behind or in front, to wave at someone way down the row, or just for the sake of popping. Teachers tried sporadically to establish a bit of order, but all their attempts, whether wimpy or harsh, were mostly ineffectual.

Clinging to my life preserver on this turbulent sea, I spotted a few randomly sprinkled islands of calm—soothing, gracious, and inviting—like pictures in a travel brochure. These were classes from Catholic, Christian, and other private schools. I could tell by their uniforms. But more than that, I could tell because they were sitting calmly in their seats.

Pulling out my opera glasses, I scrutinized them carefully. Like a scientific observer on a fact-finding mission, I had questions. What set these children apart? Why were they able to sit still? Were they unhappy? Afraid to be themselves? Had they been threatened with punishment?

Not as far as I could see. Instead, they seemed like normal, happy children, perhaps even happier than the ones in constant motion. They weren't sitting in silence, but were chatting with those nearest them, some girls comparing jewelry or smoothing their hair—much the same as adults waiting for a performance. Their teachers were not watching them like hawks or prison guards; neither did they seem harried or overburdened or as if preparing for the next outbreak.

The longer I watched, the clearer it became that these children, in general, seemed to be self-governed rather than dependent on the adults around them to keep them in line. It occurred to me that while the disruptive children seemed to have more freedom, actually the self-governed children had the truest freedom of all—the freedom to govern themselves and their own actions.

What made the difference? How did some children become self-governing, while others were so dependent on outside control? Long after the first and last notes of the concert sounded, and in many quiet moments in the days ahead, I thought about the grown-up lesson I had unexpectedly encountered at the Lollipop Concert.

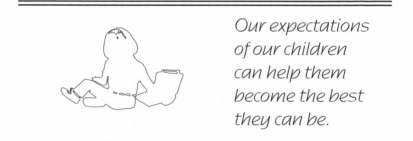

Our expectations of our children can help them become the best they can be.

A Word about Expectations

Popular wisdom tells us that people rise to the level of expectation of those above. In factories and business, when companies expect more of employees, production and customer service are better. On fields, courts, and in arenas, coaches demand the best to produce star athletes.

In a similar way, our expectations of our children can help them become the best they can be. Expectation is vital to our vision of where our children are headed. It's not so much that we decide we want Johnny to be a rocket scientist or Megan to be an Olympic ice skater. We're talking about something more subtle and more important than career goals. We're talking about the kind of men and women we are preparing for the future.

Our training of their character and the day-to-day progress we make in helping them build it—that's where our expectations can and should be of the highest.

Children have a God-given potential for self-control. The sensitive period to begin this lifelong process is in the toddler years. But before we can do anything to see it released, we need to examine our own attitudes and expectations. Then we can make adjustments wherever necessary to help our children become the kind of people God wants them to be.

First, we need to put aside any preconceived ideas concerning children's capabilities and limitations. As a starting point, try mentally stepping back in time, or perhaps around the world, to think about what has been required of children in other times and other places. In many societies, children are given responsibility and treated as adults well before adolescence. Earlier in our own culture, children worked and participated fully in adult social life. Our current society is actually an exception in having created such a distinctly defined and prolonged period of childhood.

Here, we're looking for a more balanced view, one not bound to our own culture, which for years has been expecting less and less from children and is already paying the price. Yes, perhaps there were times when children were raised too rigidly, but our pendulum seems to have swung too far the other way. Now it seems anything goes: "After all, they're only children."

Is it only coincidence that as our standards for children have collapsed, we no longer see the Abraham Lincolns and George Washington Carvers we once produced in America?

Maybe we need to stop looking at them as "only children" and start seeing that they are our future, our inheritance, and the parents of the generations to come.

Maybe it's time to take the idea of self-control out of storage and give it a good polishing. Is there something important we've been missing? Is there value in a row of children sitting calmly while waiting for a concert? What does it matter in the long run? And what does it have to do with producing men and women of integrity?

Let's go back and start at the beginning.

The Development of Motor Control

Turn your thoughts to the first months of watching your baby grow. Remember when his arms waved aimlessly, just moving for the joy of movement? You hung eye-catching things in front of him, and over time, his arms' wide circles narrowed in scope, becoming more purposeful, until finally his hand made contact.

Even if this was a random event, the result was entertaining and definitely worth repeating. Gradually your baby perfected his aim. As he did so, he was exercising both his brain and his body—more particularly, the messages and coordination between the two. Soon he was 100 percent accurate in batting the toy. What child development specialists call "gross motor control" was being developed through concentrating on a target and practicing. (We will discuss concentration thoroughly in the next chapter.)

The Difference between Gross and Fine Motor Control

Over the next few years, you witnessed (or will witness) the refinement of your child's motor control from gross to fine. Where gross motor control is waving a rattle, fine motor control is picking up a Cheerio with a sticky finger and putting it in his mouth or capturing a tiny feather and twisting his hand to examine it from every angle. To properly develop both gross and fine motor control, a child must be developmentally ready and must have an environment that offers opportunities to practice.

My son Jonathan, who has Down's syndrome and is four years old as I write, has given me the opportunity to study more closely the intricacies of this process. Other children make progress in leaps and bounds. We take their development for granted. With children like Jonathan, every part of the process takes on greater individual significance as we are required to put more thought, care, and practice into helping him achieve each small developmental step. From lifting his head to sitting to walking to climbing the stairs— each skill has taken infinitely more hours of practice to achieve.

Observing Jonathan has also shown me that gross motor skill is virtually indispensable to fine motor. Because he was delayed in his ability to sit on his own, Jonathan was not able to use his arms to play as a sitting baby would; with no practice, his fine motor control would have been even more delayed. To compensate, we sat him up with his back straight, while encouraging him to hold light rattles. Thus, when the time came for him to feed himself, he was strong enough to lift a spoon because of all his early practice.

From Motor Control to Self-Control

There are parallels between the young child's development of motor control and his later potential for developing self-control:

From gross motor control to fine. A child progresses from the big and obvious movements to the smaller and subtler— one builds a foundation for the other. A child developing self-control follows a similar pattern.

Needing practice to make perfect. Just as in motor development, the child needs opportunities to exercise his limited powers of self-control to prepare him to gracefully handle the unexpected.

69

Reflecting the level of expectations. Did you know that when children with Down's syndrome were raised in institutions, the average age at which they learned to walk was seven? Now, raised in loving homes, with parents whose expectations are higher, they learn to walk at two. This is parallel to the development of self-control in the child. In general, children rise to the level of expectation of their parents and teachers.

Expectations influence a child's long-range level of performance. Also, as in the concert example, they can affect specific behavior.

In day-to-day situations—at home or when going to the grocery store, church, or the library—my husband and I have found one small thing to be of enormous benefit. We let our children know clearly beforehand what our expectations are for their behavior.

For example, on our way to church, we remind them that there will be only one trip to the bathroom—before the service starts; that we will be sitting together as a family; that we expect them to sit still, listen attentively, and participate fully; that they should refrain from rattling their bulletins or bothering those around us with unnecessary noise; that when the time comes to leave for Sunday School, they are to walk, not run; that they are to treat their Sunday School teachers with respect and other children with courtesy; that they are not to overdo it at the hospitality table; that they are not to disappear when it's time to go home.

When they know what is expected, all it takes is a glance at someone who is out of order—you know the glance I mean. Not a glance that instills fear, just one that reminds them where they are and what the expectation is.

This is part of the process of teaching children to become self-governing rather than needing to be kept in line moment to moment by adults.

How to Foster Self-Control

Be Realistic

In studying independence and order, we took the long view to see how developing those potentials would help our children as teenagers and adults. With the attribute of self-control, I hardly need to persuade you that this will be of great benefit to your child later on.

But I do need to emphasize two areas of caution. First, we need to make sure that what we are aiming for in our children is genuine self-control, not conduct based on fear of punishment. Although in the younger years, a child's behavior is controlled through discipline and respect for authority, we are seeking at the same time to develop the child's ability to govern himself. Even if a child's behavior is consistently good, if it is always the result of control by others, he will be vulnerable to rebellion when he is older.

The second caution is this: Construct your expectations realistically. Children are individuals, and to make things even more complicated, they're changing all the time. You need to know your child well and to have an accurate picture of his capabilities. Observe, observe, observe! Set your expectations high, but never too high for your child to reach. Otherwise you end up with a discouraged child.

Remember, as Christian parents we need to rely on God's help; we can ask for and receive His guidance in setting our expectations and in helping our children to meet them.

Begin Early

Keep in mind that each of these potentials—independence, order, self-control, and those we've yet to discuss—do not exist in isolation. There is an interplay and balance among them. Thus, when you provide your child with an orderly environment and opportunities to develop independence, you are also providing the best setting for developing his self-control.

Pouring his own milk and carrying his cereal bowl to the table require independence, a sense of order, and a lot of self-control. The more often you turn this sort of activity over to him, the more practice he will get. But also, just as you hung rattles in front of your child to teach him to reach specifically, you can provide your child with motivation and specific practice in the art of self-control.

Start with gross motor control. Use a balance beam or walking on a line (simply a line of masking tape on the floor) to introduce your child to the concept of bringing his body under control. Show how staying on the beam or the line requires careful, slow, thoughtful movement.

Once your child has practiced and gained confidence with this, try the next exercise to challenge and refine his growing sense of self-control: walking with a bell.

A glass bell is ideal, because the clapper is easy to see, or look for a bell where the clapper is visible below the rim of the bell. Have your child sit across the room from you. If you have more than one child, have them sit in a large circle. Atmosphere is important: The room should be still, the mood quietly dramatic. Show the bell, drawing the children's attention to the clapper. Hold the bell with one hand, a little above waist level, arm comfortably bent but leading. Now, slowly and oh-so-carefully, begin walking toward your child. Exaggerate the care you are taking to keep the bell from ringing (remember, it will be much harder for him!). Keep your eyes on the bell. Standing in front of your child, signal him to stand, give him the bell carefully, without ringing it. Then return to sit while he carries the bell back to you or to someone else in the circle. Attention should be riveted on the clapper. The unintentional ringing of the bell provides instant feedback to the child to move more carefully. The child is reminded that he can, with a little effort, have more control over his movement.[1]

Build Integrity

Would it be stretching the point to think that such simple exercises in the early years could prepare our children for more mature challenges later on? Christian parents may see similarities between the line on the floor and the straight and narrow path we follow; between the bell ringing and the nudge of the Holy Spirit when we need to get back on track.

Small beginnings are important ones. The child's first lessons in self-control are meant to give him a clear sense that he is master over one thing—his body. Later, he will extend that mastery to his plans, emotions, and even thoughts.

Think about it: As adults and parents, we are stewards over much. By contrast, our children begin with nothing but their own bodies. I challenge my own children by telling them clearly that their own bodies are the first thing given to them by God to learn to govern. When they are fidgety and restless, I remind them they are in control: "You are the boss of your own body. You can tell it what to do."

From their first words on, our children are expected to use care in what they say and how they say it. Bad language, name calling, sarcasm, or put-downs of others—none of that is tolerated. We teach our children that each person is precious to God and that our treatment of others should reflect this. Our expectations are high because we feel this is central to the harmony in our home.[2]

As our children mature, they can and should be challenged to extend their control—for instance, in their reactions to life's frustrations. They need to learn that ending up with an extra buttonhole at the neck is not cause for a major breakdown, but simply a signal to unbutton and rebutton the shirt properly.

To teach them well, as in the other areas, we model the appropriate behaviors. That means that we treat others (including our children) with kindness and that we learn to handle stress with graciousness. Isn't it interesting how helping our children realize their potential begins to help us realize our own?

Perhaps the finest area of self-control, comparable to the most refined motor skill, would be the control we develop of our thoughts. I'm not speaking of repressing emotions but of learning how to think constructively and positively, of allowing God to use all things for good. We can begin early with our children to steer them away from feelings of being a victim or blaming others. We can sympathize with their trials while teaching them to take responsibility for their responses. Above all, we need to discourage our children from making excuses for unacceptable behavior.

When society lowers its expectations, murmuring, "After all, they're only children," a pattern is established of making excuses. We end with condoms being handed out in high schools, backed by a pathetic "They're only teenagers. How can we expect them to be abstinent?" As parents of young children, we can begin now to bring up our children with a higher standard.

The seeds of self-control need to be watered early to produce what they were meant to produce: responsibility, integrity, self-government, and self-esteem. We want our children to experience lives well lived, lives with no excuses. Begin by preparing them when they are young.

❦

Like a city whose walls are broken down
is a man who lacks self-control.
Proverbs 25:28

Chapter Nine

Concentration:
"Quiet! Mind at Work!"

Pausing on her way to the laundry room, Diane gave her three-year-old daughter, Monica, an encouraging pat. "I'm so glad you like those new sewing cards," she said, smiling.

Diane had found the set while exploring a nearby teachers' store and had finally found time to show them to Monica yesterday. With only a few minutes before dinner, they had had time to "sew" only one card together. Then they had placed the materials back in the box and put the box on the shelf.

This morning, after breakfast, Monica had made a bee-line for the sewing cards. She had chosen the orange lace and was carefully looping it through the holes around the yellow fish. Now she looked up and smiled briefly at her mom, returning absorbed to her "sewing." Diane watched silently for a few minutes, ready to help Monica fine-tune her efforts if necessary. But Monica was doing well on her own, so Diane left. Mounds of laundry beckoned.

Doesn't the laundry always take longer than you think? A considerable chunk of time had passed before Diane emerged from the laundry room. *Better check on Monica,* she thought. The now-completed orange-bordered yellow fish was prominently displayed on the table. Monica had begun a blue flower with a purple lace.

Throughout the morning, as Diane finished each of her own chores, she returned to check on Monica's progress. Most of the time, Monica barely noticed her mother's presence. It seemed that the longer she "sewed," the more absorbed she became.

Finally all the cards were finished for Mom to admire. "Here, let's put them on the counter for Daddy to see when he comes home," Diane said.

"But, Mommy, can't I do them again?"

"Well, what about some of the other things on your shelves? Do you want to use the peg board? How about a puzzle?"

Diane couldn't believe that Monica, who had already spent over an hour with the sewing cards, would want to do them again. Besides, the shelves were brimming over with great materials. It just didn't seem right to spend so much time on one thing.

But Monica was determined. She wanted to redo all that she had done. Diane sighed, helped her unlace the laces, and then left her on her own to do the cards again.

The next morning, when Monica went straight to the same shelf for the same work, her mother tried to steer her toward something new, again without success.

As Monica happily sewed at her little table, Diane called to tell me about the problem she was having. She was worried that her daughter's development was slowing down. "I mean, she has all these other wonderful things to choose, and she only wants to use the sewing cards. Should I make her do something else? Is it really okay for her to do the same thing over and over again?"

How Children Learn

Diane asked that question because she is an adult, and the way we live our lives is so different from the child's way. Our own fast-paced, responsibility-laden days make it possible to allot only a certain amount of time to any one activity. Most of us have forgotten what it is like to spend as much time as we want on one particular thing; now the time we spend doing something we enjoy is governed by how much time we can afford.

Children do not live this way. And though the clash in our respective tempos can be frustrating, aren't you glad God gave us children to remind us how it used to be? I love to catch one of my children lost in learning something. I may not be sure what the lesson is; but if a child is concentrating, I can be sure something is being built into him that will help him in the future, though it may be simply the ability to focus and concentrate.

Consider Concentration

The sensitive period for concentration occurs during the toddler years. It's a quiet drive rather than a powerful one. If independence is like a rushing river—carrying along everything in its path—concentration is more like a meandering brook. Not really concerned with getting where it's going, it follows an indirect path, picking up water from other sources and gaining momentum until it becomes a dependable, consistent stream. Here, obstacles must be removed and logjams broken to prevent the flow from being hindered.

Translated into practical terms, we need to help our children develop concentration by removing distractions and encouraging its growth into a strong and vital current.

You have already seen concentration in your child. Remember how your baby focused on the mobile above his crib or changing table even before he could touch it? Think of how he followed it with his eyes, concentration straining his whole body toward the bright objects above.

Remember when he found his hand? Remember how he held it at arm's distance and studied it for endless moments of baby time? How long could an adult hold his arm up in the air without tiring, even if he could experience the same sort of fascination with his fingers?

That's how the child's concentration is. It's spontaneous and surprising. It is not something you can make happen, but something you stumble upon. Once you discover it, you want to remember where to find it, though, because you want to encourage your child to spend as much time as he can there, bringing out the intensity of focus he showed when he discovered his own hand.

The Value of Choice

You cannot force a child to concentrate, but you can maximize his opportunities. By knowing your child well through thoughtful observation, you can learn those things that bring out the focus in him. When he chooses them spontaneously, be supportive. When he needs help finding something to do, remember to offer options that have focused his attention in the past.

When the child chooses his own work, it is more likely he will bring his full attention to it.

In the preschool years, it's especially important for children to choose their own activities. In the example of Monica and her mother, Monica was on the right track, choosing her own work, rather than depending on her mother for direction.

Choice is also obviously linked with independence, but I bring it up here for a very specific reason: When the child chooses his own work, it is more likely he will bring his full attention to it.

The ability to choose does not come naturally. However, you can begin to cultivate it from the earliest years. Even before your child can dress himself, give him a choice between a blue shirt or a red shirt.[1] As he begins to catch on, he can graduate to three or four choices. At some point—ideally, by the time he has learned to dress himself—he will have become capable of choosing from all his own clothes. Help make that possible by making sure that his dresser drawers are the right height and easy to open. Bring his closet rack down to his level.

Find ways to let him choose the order in which to do things: Do you want to take your bath or brush your teeth first? The cat had her kittens; whom should we call first— Grandma or Daddy at work?

By cultivating choice as part of his everyday life, you will teach your child how to exercise his will within appropriate limits. Before he even begins school, you should see the results: a child who chooses his own work and works independently. And remember, for all the reasons we mentioned before, this is most likely the child who will also be able to concentrate.

How to Foster Concentration

Encourage Repetition

A child who repeats activities is exhibiting strong concentration. Monica's eagerness to lace the sewing cards again and again gave solid indication that she had great potential for learning. She might as well have been wearing a big sign that said: "Quiet! Mind at Work!"

Once Diane understood this concept, she saw her daughter's activities from a different perspective. She realized that along with encouraging Monica to choose her activities, she could help her daughter further by allowing her to spend as much time as she wanted concentrating on one particular thing.

Repetition is always something to encourage; it helps the child develop his potential for concentration. It also means learning is taking place. So, for example, when your child finishes a puzzle, before scooping it up and putting it away, ask if he would like to do it again. If he has stacked a tower of nesting cups, ask if he would like to mix them up and build again.

Contrary to what we might assume in our often hectic society, a child who spends all morning on one or two activities is showing more learning potential than one who flits from one activity to the next. Do all you can to encourage your child to slow down and stick with something for a while.

Find the Window

Also closely tied with concentration is self-control, for a child who can't sit still will have a hard time focusing on anything. Here is a clear case of "bringing the body so the mind will follow." The exercises introduced in the previous chapter, walking on a line or walking with a bell, serve not only to perfect your child's self-control, but also to sharpen his concentration skills. Through being challenged to bring his best to each exercise, he comes closer to realizing his potential.

Even the bounciest child will have at least one thing that will open the window of concentration. I know because I have one of the most in-motion children in the world! In addition to blessing me in many other ways, Sophia has taken me to the limit of my assumptions about children; but even Sophia finally succumbed to something that released her potential to concentrate: coloring books.

Many years ago, I misunderstood coloring books; I never had them in the house. When my first two daughters received them as gifts, I threw them away. As a zealous, protective young mother, I was just certain that coloring in the lines would destroy my children's creativity.

I know better now. It would take much more than a mere coloring book to stifle the creative impulse of a young child. Coloring books have definite merit. In addition to helping perfect fine motor control, they have an almost unequaled power to captivate the complete attention of even the most distractible child.

And so, when I found Sophia for the first time poised over the pages of a coloring book, oblivious to the comings and goings of the rest of our larger-than-life family, I think I shouted, "Hallelujah!"

Sophia is still much the same—a bobbing blond in almost perpetual motion. But I have the assurance that she can concentrate. She still uses her coloring books, but now she has learned to concentrate on other things as well.

Use Challenging Activities

Concentration is a portable skill. Once the child's ability to concentrate has been evoked through one activity, he is better able to focus on others. That's why it's so important that when he finds something that absorbs his interest, you allow him to focus on that activity.

In addition to observing those unique activities that release your own child's potential for concentration, you can also use routine activities to challenge him.

For instance, show him in slow and exaggerated detail how to close a door without a sound. Show how turning the knob brings the latch in, how it is possible to hold the knob in such a way so as to release the latch only when the door is completely closed. Ask him to take a turn. Challenge him to carry a chair or stool across the room and set it down, again without a sound. With the utmost concentration, setting down one leg at a time, it is possible.

This distinction between sound and silence is a great place to sharpen your child's powers of concentration. Sit together, with eyes closed (the better to concentrate), and list the noises you hear. In the most quiet room of your house (uncarpeted), show him a pin, and ask him to close his eyes and tell you when he hears it drop.

Another tool is the Silence Game: Gather your children and together create the most quiet place possible. Turn off the phone, draw the blinds or curtains. Tiptoe and whisper. Then sit with them cross-legged on the floor, making sure there is a space around each. As you tell them how the game is played, let your voice gradually drop to the smallest whisper. By the end, your children should be using their utmost powers of concentration to hear you.

"We're going to play the Silence Game. I'm going to tiptoe very quietly into the kitchen. You should close your eyes and listen very carefully. You'll need to hold your body perfectly still to hear me. I'm going to whisper your name. When you hear me whisper, come out without a sound. Remember, I'm going to whisper so quietly you can hardly hear me."

After the last barely audible words, silently leave. Pause. Then from the next room, whisper the names of each of your children, starting with the ones least likely to hold still.

There is a parallel here between this Small Beginnings exercise and our lives as adults. Waiting for your parent's whisper as a child is a lot like the stillness we need later on to discern any impression our Heavenly Father might want to make on our hearts. The Silence Game is early preparation for that stillness.

As you begin to observe your child concentrating and watch his potential develop, you will yourself develop a deeper appreciation for the role it will play in his life now and later on.

Concentration is one of the potentials built into your child that enables him to become all that God designed him to be. Concentration is also an invaluable key that will unlock many doors of opportunity; it is the key to your child's ability to learn. The child who can concentrate, who can focus completely, who can devote himself completely to a task, will thrive in an academic environment. As an adult, he will be able to bring his best to any task and therefore be better equipped to make a significant contribution.

Use the activities above, but also pay special attention to the Small Beginnings exercises coming up in part 3. They were specifically designed to evoke your child's ability to concentrate. They can help you put this important key to learning in your child's hand.

❧

Better one handful with tranquility
than two handfuls with toil
and chasing after the wind.
Ecclesiastes 4:6

Chapter Ten

Service: "Let Me Help!"

Anyone who dropped by unannounced yesterday morning would have known in a flash we have a lot of children. Voices from every direction—the early birds cheerful, the slower risers still trying to track down books and sweaters. Contrasting rhythms of feet bumping up and down the stairs. Washer whooshing, kettle whistling, three-ring binders clicking shut. Cabinet doors opening to receive last night's dinner dishes and offer this morning's cereal bowls.

It was the usual controlled pandemonium as six children prepared themselves, their breakfasts, and their lunches—while juggling morning chores and extra help for two toddlers who need a little and two babies who need a lot.

Wait a minute. Did I say morning chores? Taking care of the younger children? Maybe it sounds like quite enough—way beyond the norm—that the children were taking care of themselves rather than relying on Mom. Is it possible to expect so much of children on a daily basis?

Discover the Gift of Service

I want to help you discover that it is not only possible but essential that you teach your children to serve. In addition to showing you how to do it, I want to illustrate how instilling an attitude of teamwork among all family members will enrich each individual and the family as a whole.

The gift of serving others is an integral part of the Christian life. In serving, we look beyond our own needs to meet those of others. This is a distinctive that sets us apart and truly enables our light to shine. Loving service is the example Christ set for us. I believe it is the key to true satisfaction in life.

But does this relate to toddlers? Absolutely. The desire to serve is a potential God has built into each of us. So why do younger children clamor to help while older children are often lazy and resentful?

We've seen it already, with independence, order, and concentration. Just as with the other sensitive periods, the desire to serve emerges and is strongest during the toddler years. For it to be released fully, it must be encouraged at the appropriate time, when it first begins. A child who is not given opportunities to serve early on will be the one who balks at serving when it is required from him later.

Unlike the other sensitive periods, which can be developed in a classroom setting, the seeds of service find their most fertile soil in the home. In the family, God has provided a unique training ground for this potential.

Even if you're reading this with your first baby still in your arms, it's not too early to be thinking of making service a priority. It's never too soon to develop a vision for your family. What kind of home do you want for your children? Is it really possible to raise children who think of others more than themselves? How can we get them started?

Start Them Young

Yesterday's morning visitor would have seen an amazing and delightful sight: four-year-old Jonathan (who, because he has Down's syndrome, is developmentally more like a two-year-old) hauling a small trash basket down the hall. The basket was full, and so was my heart—to the brim.

He was so proud of himself because he knew he had taken a big step. He had often seen his brothers collecting the baskets to empty into the big container in the garage. And because Jonathan looks up to his brothers, he wanted to do it too.

Can you imagine what would have happened if, thinking him too young, I had taken the basket and emptied it myself? Of course, I knew there was a chance he would spill the basket. But what was most important here was not efficiency, but nurturing my son's potential for service—and the sense of joy the young child feels when he is useful.

The last thing a spontaneously helping child needs is an adult hovering and worrying over him. Instead, I had Zachary, now eight, get another full basket to accompany Jonathan to the garage. There, the boys finished their mission together and then put the baskets away.

With eleven children, our family has reached the point where it has become much easier to instill a love of service because the younger children have so many role models. Remember, your first child may one day be the oldest of a multitude; but whether he is the oldest of ten or two, what you have developed in him will serve to set the tone and example for any that follow. Make sure you teach him well—he's a major investment in the future of all your children.

An only child especially needs to be encouraged to serve, to feel that his help is needed. This may take extra effort from parents who could easily do it all without their child's help.

As in so many areas of our children's development, the first challenge is ourselves. We don't want to limit our children with popular trends. Do our attitudes need adjustment? A mental tour of other cultures should provide ample illustration that our own has a distinctly different pattern for childhood.

My children are fascinated looking through *National Geographic* to find pictures of African girls walking back to their village with the day's catch—bearing a stack of shiny silver fish on their heads! Mexican children help their mothers pound the corn to make tortillas. Children all over the globe sweep huts, fetch water, hang clothes to dry, tote their younger siblings for busy parents.

In many countries, young boys learn their trades by their fathers' sides. Even in our own country, children growing up on ranches and farms help milk cows, shear sheep, bale hay, plant, and harvest.

But for most families in our country, the trend toward fewer children and more household conveniences has meant a decline in responsibility for children. In fact, people from other times and places might say our children were somewhat pampered and spoiled. Perhaps we need to expect a little more? Or maybe we just need to start looking at the children themselves and take our cue from them. Jonathan carrying the trash out may have been a personal first, but it was only the most recent in a growing list of household chores he has shown an interest in. And believe me, in our house, when someone shows an interest in a chore, it's theirs to keep—until a younger one comes along to take over. In fact, in our family as soon as you can stand, you can serve.

Toddlers love to help and feel honored to have something to do. Why not learn to think on their terms, to find ways to let them be useful? They need to know they are an important part of the family. Sometimes I wonder if a lot of crankiness in little children could be averted by making them feel less unimportant.

What, after all, can a toddler do? It doesn't come easily to most adults to turn things over to those who are slower and less competent. At first, parents need a little reflection, careful planning, and patience to put some of these Small Beginnings ideas into practice.

In appendix B, you will find a list of age-appropriate chores. When you see something like peeling carrots listed under two to three years old, you may be skeptical. And certainly, if you hand your toddler a carrot and a peeler, he is as likely to peel his hand as the carrot. But if you are prepared to teach him, he is ready to learn. I recommend that you read chapters 11 and 12 to prepare yourself to teach any age-appropriate activity to your toddler. These few simple techniques will go a long way to helping you become the best teacher your child will ever have. Use housework as your training ground.

Housework 101

At the doctor's office or the zoo, in grocery aisles or church parking lots, for years I've been answering questions. It starts with: "Are those all your children?" Then, no matter what direction the conversation has taken, it usually ends with the Big Question: "How do you manage?"

You become the best teacher your child will ever have.

We figured things out gradually. After all, we started with one or two children ourselves. While it's no secret that big families have a high degree of efficiency, it's because we have to. But mothers of many ("grandmultiparas" is what we're called by OB-GYNs) would be the first to admit we're not smarter, just responding to a desperate situation—we're outnumbered.

Still, I think any family can benefit from what we've learned. And even the smallest family can use big-family techniques to make their own lives more manageable. In addition, you will nurture in your child the potential for service, which he can carry with him wherever he goes.

Children need to feel needed. When it comes to the work necessary to manage a large household, they certainly are. In a smaller family, Mom might be able to do everything for everybody. But is that really what you want? Then not only would you be frustrated and tired, but burdened with a houseful of spoiled children, thinking only of themselves and not of others.

Try a Team Approach

Look at your housework as belonging to all members of the family. Housework is something of enormous benefit that should take as little time as possible.

I remind my children that if one of us cleans the house, it might take six hours, but if six of us work together, it will take only one. Then we all have more time for the fun things, and Mom can join in the fun too.

Try a team approach: Use ten-minute pick-ups throughout the day to avoid being left with monumental messes when you're tired enough to drop.[1]

On housecleaning day, get everyone involved (see appendix B for age-appropriate chores). I give my kids a chance to choose what they're going to do—"I'll vacuum upstairs," "I'll sweep and dust," "I'll clean the kitchen"—and then turn them loose. Only when they balk do I start giving assignments.

Organize everything with shared housework in mind. A stool in the laundry room means even the shortest family members can help fold clothes. Dishes on the bottom shelves enable a three-year-old to put away dishes or a four-year-old to set the table without help.

Keep cleaning supplies secure from roving toddlers; but once you have taught older children how to use them safely, make them accessible to those older children. Make them user-friendly. My ten-year-old, Benjamin, took more of a shine to cleaning the bathroom when I put the essentials in a special rubber tote with handle.

Especially if you have boys, be sure to watch Don Aslett's video on housecleaning (see appendix A). His techniques are a treasure, his humor is a breath of fresh air, and his enthusiasm is contagious. Besides, seeing a man as a housecleaning expert will add new appeal for the males of the house.

A Word about Chore Charts

What about chore charts? I can only offer my own experience. My husband (wonderful man) once sought to improve our household routine by making a chore chart. It was an artful affair, a blue nubby flannel board with clear vinyl pockets (one per child) holding chore cards he had prepared with calligraphy and stickers of vacuums, beds, dishes, brooms, etc. My job was to divvy up the cards each morning, checking later to make sure the children had done their work.

Sounds like just the thing a big family would need, doesn't it? But things aren't always as they seem. In our house the chore chart wreaked havoc. The children rapidly became territorial and argumentative about their chores ("Mo-om, I did the dishes yesterday!" "Why do I have more things to do?"). Besides the ugliness of their worrying about their share and what was fair, I also was spending more time in organization and follow-through.

We eventually took down the chore chart and went back to what had always worked (lending credibility to the old saw, "If it works, don't fix it"). What works for us is flexibility and spontaneity. What works is when I can ask someone to do something that needs to be done without hearing, "But that's not on the chore chart!" What works is when my children respond to my requests by taking responsibility without a lot of fuss and comparison.

Different methods work for different families. If the chart method works for you, then use it. (If you want to try it for a few days, call my husband and borrow ours.) If it doesn't work, don't be disappointed or hard on yourself. Whatever you do, don't use a chore chart if it becomes more of a burden than a blessing. Keep in mind the big picture.

Our goal is children with hearts of generosity and not measuring who did what. Build this heart of service from the early years. As your children grow in competence and confidence, continue to introduce new skills. Our children, looking up to the next older, have a sense of "graduating" to the next level of chores. That's a powerful motivator.

Our goal is children with hearts of generosity.

But start early. Include your toddler on the cleanup team, even if so far your team is just Mom and Dad. Give him a dust cloth—it will keep him busy by your side, a far more valuable endeavor than dumping Cheerios on the floor in the kitchen!

Four Questions

I didn't like divvying up the chore cards, but I do have four guidelines for how I distribute work as part of our daily routine. Actually, they are four questions you can ask yourself about anything that needs to be done.

Can he do it himself? Is your child able to dress himself? To clean his room? To clean up his own place after breakfast? Then he should. This first question is related to independence, and though it does not mean that you should be rigid (it is OK and a good model to help others), the rule of thumb is this: If he can do it himself, let him.

Can someone younger do it? In an amazing display of toddler-size service, my Madeleine and Jonathan (three and four, re-spectively) began a year ago to take the plastic cups and sau-cers out of the dishwasher in the morning and put them away in the cabinets. The older children are responsible for the more difficult items. And probably, Madeleine and Jonathan are looking forward to one day taking over the more ad-vanced chore.

There are chores even the smallest can do. Don't ask your eight-year-old to bring a diaper for the baby if your three-year-old is around. The younger child will relish the opportunity to serve, and the older child is capable of more advanced assignments. For big cleanups and small, work is distributed according to one principle: Delegate any task to the youngest capable of doing it.

Can it be done differently? You may have grown up with a mother who was so perfect she ironed the sheets. Or maybe she didn't iron the sheets, and your friend's mother did; and you wondered why your mother didn't. Anywhere along the line, you may have picked up some ideas of per-fection that just aren't adding much to your life.

Ever hear the story about the young wife who argued with her husband each Thanksgiving because she cut the turkey in half to roast it? When he insisted that it wasn't necessary, she asked her mother why she'd grown up with Thanksgiv-ing turkeys cut in half. Mom, who couldn't remember see-ing a whole turkey in her own childhood, had to go to Grandma to find out why. Grandma was amazed at the leg-acy she had passed on. And so were her daughter and granddaughter when she told them that she'd always cut the turkey in half because her oven was too small and each year's turkey too big to cook the normal way.

What doesn't fit in your oven? Are you doing things in ways that are unnecessary or too exacting for your family?

Here's a personal example—again, based on my eternal laundry situation. Early in my motherhood, I began to notice that children have a tough time keeping clothes neatly folded in their drawers. For a while I was frustrated at the time I had wasted folding. Then it occurred to me that folding could be a much more informal affair than I had ever imagined.

This will explain my current, casual routine: As I empty the dryer, I quickly and just barely fold big items—jeans, T-shirts, pajamas—in stacks, one per child. The children periodically come and get their stacks to put away in their rooms. In the meantime, the small items of clean laundry—socks, underwear, napkins—accumulate in the laundry basket until it threatens to overflow. Just before it does, I call all the children, turn on some music, and dump the clothes onto the carpeted floor of my bedroom. They fold together until the basket is empty; then everyone puts everything away.

I use this chore as an example and share it in such detail to reveal how chores don't have to be done the way your mother did them or the way your neighbor does them; they can instead be tailored to your family, keeping your priorities in mind. With the laundry, my goal was to get a very large and very necessary job done without any unnecessary stress, while promoting the joy of serving together as a family.

My choice involved modifying my standards about how folded clothes should look. But it was a choice I made willingly. Since nine of my children are under thirteen, most of them are not capable of folding to perfection. But, as I said, clothes in children's drawers never seem to stay folded for long. And I've noticed wrinkled T-shirts have a way of smoothing out when my boys put them on.

Keep in mind that modifying your standards is not always a sign of laziness, but sometimes of intelligent decision making. When we lower our standards because circumstances defeat us or we feel weak, we don't feel good about the result. But when we evaluate the demands on our time, our children's capabilities, and our family's priorities, a decision to temporarily modify our standards in some area may actually be the most responsible path, which leads me to the last question concerning housework:

Does it need to be done at all? When my fifth child came along, I began streamlining what I thought was necessary. The process went something like this: "Do the dishes need to be hand-dried and put away immediately, or can they air-dry overnight?" The must-do's that were dropped were evidently of such small consequence that I can't even remember the others.

Receive each child's personal best as though it were the best.

A writer writes best from experience, and this was mine: I wanted my house to look nice. I wanted a lot of children. Though not mutually exclusive desires, pursuing both created some tension. Resolving that tension involved some compromise. Reaching that compromise took some time.

The principle that housework belongs to the whole family was always a priority. And that involved compromise, as well. For example, if I want my nine-year-old to vacuum, I need to understand that his result—even when he works to the best of his ability—will not look the same as mine.

Keeping that in mind, you can make a decision in advance to receive each child's personal best as though it were *the* best. As in my own experience of folding the clothes, this may involve lowering your standards for the finished product. That's OK. I want to assure you, as I used to assure myself, that this is one of those rare instances where lower expectations will actually serve to achieve a higher purpose.

Preparing Their Hearts for Service

While you may decide to lower your expectations regarding the appearance of your house—or the folded clothes—I urge you to set your expectations higher regarding your children's *attitude* toward service.

This is another of those culture-based issues well worth examining. Our society values some types of work more highly than others. Though this may be the way of the world, this is not the way of Christ.

When our Christian values are at odds with the world's, it is our responsibility as parents to weigh the difference and carefully consider how to pass on what is right to our children. In addition, our children must see that we ourselves live out what we are teaching them.

My view is this: Jesus modeled a life of service. He gave everything, no holding back. He preached to thousands at the Sermon on the Mount, but He also washed His disciples' feet. This shows me that all service is pleasing to God, that He doesn't attach greater status to one form than another. More important than the service is the heart of the one who serves.

In practical terms, this means changing a diaper—if done in the proper spirit—is as important as negotiating a peace treaty. If I want my children to have a Christlike attitude toward service, I begin by modeling it myself. This is one area where actions definitely do speak louder than words.

Prepare Your Own Heart First

As in so many other aspects of being a parent, the first step in preparing your children's hearts for service is to prepare your own. Pray for God to show you the areas where your own attitude needs adjustment. When you find an attitude toward work that's robbing you of joy—perfectionism, balking, resentfulness—ask God to help you change. He will. And haven't you already been surprised at how much

easier it is to change negative attitudes when you're thinking of your children?

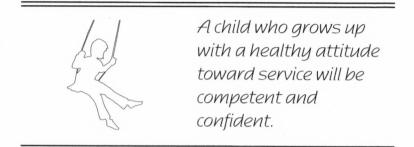

*A child who grows up
with a healthy attitude
toward service will be
competent and
confident.*

Find the joy in your own daily work, so your children can
find joy in what you ask them to do. Give your best and they
will give their best. Appendix C contains "A Spoonful of
Scripture," verses that should inspire and encourage both
you and your children.

Use Biblical Examples and Teachings

The New Testament is filled with stories of service, of
those who gave from the heart: The Good Samaritan, Mary
breaking the alabaster jar to anoint Jesus, Jesus Himself giving all for us. Share these with your children (see appendix
A for toddler resources). As your child grows, you will be
able to use these stories to show your children how to apply
biblical principles in their own lives.

From the time your child is born, his character is being
formed. That's why the preschool years are so important.
Many experts feel that by the time a child is ready for
school, the kind of adult he will be is already determined.
This doesn't mean a child can't change; but after the early
years change occurs only through a concentrated application of the will. How much easier, when you think about it,
to build the best into them from the beginning!

The toddler years have quite a reputation. They are, after
all, where we see the most pure and unashamed self-

centeredness. And yet we see that God has built into each of us, like an antidote to the disease, the potential to serve. I see it when Jonathan and Madeleine want to help me fold the clothes or wash the dishes or put away the groceries.

The potential for serving others might be eclipsed by the desire to serve ourselves were it not for Jesus, who showed us the way to triumph over sin, over selfishness. Our task as parents is to give that gift to our children. The lessons begin in the early years in the home, but they will extend later into the life of the child in school, in church, and in the community. It is one thing to teach your child the Golden Rule: "Do unto others as you would have them do unto you." But the Golden Rule will remain only a concept until it has been actively applied. Opportunities to serve—especially when they involve helping those who are helpless (older children diapering babies or tying toddlers' shoes)—engrave the Golden Rule on your child's heart. And a child who lives the Golden Rule will extend the lessons beyond service and into more refined areas of manners, charity, and hospitality.

And who needs to worry about self-esteem, now a major preoccupation among worldly educators? A child who grows up with a healthy attitude toward service will be competent and confident. In my estimation, ten minutes helping Mom and feeling appreciated will build more self-esteem than a week of watching Barney!

Unselfishness: The Nature of Service

My daughter Jasmine was born six years after her older sister Samantha. For eight years Jasmine was the baby of the family. At eight, she became the middle child when her brother Joshua was born. Then, abruptly, our family pattern changed with child after child born eighteen months apart. When Samantha married, Jasmine officially became the oldest child. For years our dinner table has looked like Snow White and the seven, eight, and now nine dwarves.

Jasmine has had to work harder than most children. But she has done it with good humor and grace. She has been able to do it well because she has embraced her life and been grateful for the family God chose to place her in.

She could have taken a different path. She could have become bitter or longed for a more "normal" lifestyle. Instead, she seems to have loved almost every moment of her life. She has arrived at a spiritual maturity many adults never experience, understanding that in giving so much, she has been the one who has gained.

This year, at age twenty, Jasmine offered me six months of her life to make it possible for me to finish this book. Although she had several promising opportunities to advance her own future, she put them aside to help at home with the toddlers and newly adopted babies Jesse and Daniel. I can accept her sacrifice because I know from experience that she will end up with greater blessings than the one she has given me. That is the nature of service to others.

Jasmine, at twenty, is already experiencing a life well lived. Her secret? "If you want to be treated like a servant, act like a princess. If you want to be treated like a princess, act like a servant."

Jasmine was only eleven when she formulated her plan for a successful life. She had already found from her own experience what had been written by a wise man long ago:

A generous man will prosper;
he who refreshes others will himself be refreshed.
Proverbs 11:25

Part Three
Go!

Small Beginnings Exercises

Who said parenting would be easy? And how many people find it fun?

But the truth is, it can be much easier and a lot more fun when you learn what really makes children tick, when you're ready to relax a little and be prepared for new surprises each day.

I was surprised this morning. The early rain brought out the snails, crisscrossing our driveway with silvery, slimy trails. Just for fun, we decided to have a snail race. Each of the children chose a snail, put an identifying sticker on its back, and lined it up at a start line.

That's where we are—at the start line, ready to go. Like a marathon runner who's trained well, you feel much more prepared for the long haul. By now you may have already smoothed some bumps on the track by making some important changes at home. Most importantly, you understand the course on which you're headed. You can put your best into each day because you've seen the big picture. You've got a good idea of where you're headed.

The next two chapters will not only equip you to bring your child closer to his goals, but they will also add dimension to the adventure of being a parent. We are, after all, our children's first teachers. Many are beginning to realize that the toddler years are the most important learning years of all. That's what prompted you to pick up this book. You want to know how to make the most of this brief—but oh, so valuable—time.

Suppose we were spending some time together and I said, "Did you know that with a pair of tweezers you can help your child improve his eye-hand coordination and his ability to concentrate? Did you know that by encouraging his pincer grasp you will give him a head start on the challenge of writing well? I can even show you a special tweezer exercise that will pave the way for his future reading skills."

There's so much we can do for our children once we know a few secrets! The work you've already done is a strong foundation. Now we're ready to build on that foundation. You will discover how to create learning materials your child will enjoy and want to spend time with. You will understand the purpose behind them. You will enjoy presenting them to your child and seeing him use them on his own. And you will be rewarded as they serve in releasing your child's God-given potential.

These are the Small Beginnings exercises.

Chapter Eleven

First Things First: Creating the Exercises

Underlying Objectives

These exercises are challenging and fun for preschool children, but that won't stop older ones from trying them too! Most importantly, each will encourage and perfect certain developmental milestones. The activities may look humble and small; but as you will see, there is a lot going on beneath the surface. Hence, Small Beginnings.

We've talked about some major and often neglected aspects of development vital to a child's later ability to learn with ease. These include their independence, concentration, order, self-control, and service. You will find that the following activities are geared toward helping your children in each of these areas.

Gross and Fine Motor Control

In addition to the larger goals, the exercises also have some more specific underlying objectives: for instance, the refinement of gross and small motor control. Many of the activities call for using the pincer grasp, exercising those fine motor skills that will soon become so important to the child when he picks up a pen to learn to write.

Sensory Discrimination

Several activities focus on sensory discrimination, providing the child with an opportunity to refine his powers of discrimination using one of the five senses—sight, sound, smell, taste, or touch. These refinement exercises provide opportunities for children to sharpen their focus and expand their ability to discriminate subtle differences. This is an important foundation for later intellectual analysis.

Eye-Hand Coordination

Most of the exercises provide practice in eye-hand coordination. Also, wherever possible, they are designed to emphasize left to right movement of the hand and the eyes. This is a fundamental pattern in preparation for reading. In fact, although I am not an expert in the field of learning disabilities, I sometimes wonder if the current epidemic of dyslexia and other reading problems is the result of neglecting to provide early learning reinforcement of this simple concept.

Putting It All Together

Using what you learned in the early chapters, you will be able to read the exercises, understand the underlying objectives, and then duplicate them with similar easy-to-find materials. I also have outlined a method of presentation designed to maximize your child's ability to succeed and to obtain the built-in benefits.

Make It Possible

You will notice that the exercises are very detailed. I have broken down each operation into the smallest possible steps. As a teacher and a mother, I have found that we cannot overestimate the importance of the slightest detail in presenting an exercise to a child. The child needs to see each step clearly and understand the proper sequence of actions to achieve the purposes of each activity.

For example, in the basting exercise on pages 120–21, to accomplish the transfer of water from one side to the other, the child must clearly understand when to squeeze the baster and when to release it. This is precisely the kind of detail that has become so automatic to us, we are likely to overlook it.

A child becomes frustrated when he does not understand what we are showing him and when we can't understand why he's not learning. Sometimes this is a result of presenting something too early. Sometimes the child is not interested. But more often than not, the learning process breaks down because we have neglected attention to detail.

Golden Rule Learning

You serve your child best when you break down anything you want to teach him into a sequence of actions and then present them carefully. When we're in a hurry, we can't be sensitive to our children's needs. For the best results, take the time to put yourself in your child's place and to look at each task as if you were doing it for the first time.

By following this precept you will give your children the gift of what I call "Golden Rule Learning." This is not only an important part of the following exercises, but something that can be applied to everything we teach children—from tying shoes to peeling potatoes.

Be Creative

We all love beautiful things. Children are no different: They will be most attracted to objects that are pleasing to look at, pleasing to touch. Since we want the child to choose and enjoy using the exercises we create, we want to make every effort to make them as appealing as possible.

Actually, this will stimulate your own creativity as well. For those of you who may have thought you weren't all that creative, you will probably be very surprised at your own ingenuity once you get started.

Some Guidelines about the Exercises

Make It Complete

Each exercise is designed to be complete unto itself, all items needed for the activity in a basket or on a tray. That way, concentration is not disrupted by the need to jump up to get a sponge to clean up spills, for instance.

Make It Available

Once it has been presented, each exercise is intended to be available in a particular location, ideally a certain spot on the shelves suggested earlier. In this way your child can choose the activity independently and spend as much time as he wants. This is the practical application of the goals also discussed earlier of encouraging independence and your child's ability to choose.

If space is limited, you may rotate the exercises, keeping some tucked away and switching what is available. Or you may be able to find other interested mothers with whom to pool resources and trade back and forth. In these cases, you can help your child remember the exercise's temporary place by color-coded dots—matching ones on the shelf and the basket or tray.

It's a good idea to keep an exercise out for at least three weeks before it is removed. If your first presentation doesn't capture your child's interest, he may later change his mind.

Try It Yourself

Remember when putting together your own exercises to try everything yourself. Make sure the beads are not too big for the tweezers. Remember your child's relatively smaller hands and lack of strength and skill when testing items like tongs and basters. Squeeze sponges to see if they are too hard for little hands to wring out well. Make sure containers are child-friendly—that is, easy to open and close.

Teach Them to Be Careful

Most of us have grown up with the idea that we should keep breakables away from children. On the contrary, I would encourage you to use breakable items freely in the exercises you create. Besides being more attractive, they present the child with the challenge of being more careful in his movements.

When we prepare a child and let him use certain beautiful but breakable objects, we show that he is worthy of our trust.

We help him meet this challenge and be successful in not breaking things by being careful in the way we handle things ourselves.

Consider: How can a child learn not to break if we give him only items that can be handled carelessly with no consequences? By keeping breakables out of bounds, we send the message that we think him bound to fail. On the other hand, when we prepare a child and let him use certain beautiful but breakable objects, we show that he is worthy of our trust.

We can prepare the child by handling things with exaggerated carefulness ourselves. This draws the child's attention to the challenge of preserving something beautiful by handling it with care. Always use confident, encouraging words to remind your child to be careful.

Under these circumstances, will our children sometimes accidentally break things? Yes, once in a while, but so do we. Breaking is immediate feedback of careless movement.

A child who has been taught to be careful will certainly get the message. Breaking something is a reminder to use even more care.

Our own challenge is to accept in advance the fact that things will break and to react with graciousness when they do. That gives our children a lesson in good manners. However, I can promise that by using the principles above, you will be very surprised at how seldom things will break in your home or your classroom.

Always use confident, encouraging words to remind your child to be careful.

Finding Materials

Everything I use in my exercises has been found in places we usually go anyway: dime stores, drug stores, fabric stores, craft stores, secondhand stores, and garage sales. You may go out looking for a specific exercise, or you may come across items while looking for something else.

Small Beginnings Thinking

Why not develop the habit of Small Beginnings thinking? Then you will begin to notice useful items before you even have a specific exercise in mind. If they are bargains, buy them and put them away for later. Better yet, think of a way to use them now.

For instance, one of my key acquisitions was a smooth, round, highly polished wooden hors d'oeuvres holder—at least that's what I guessed it was—found as I was browsing through a Goodwill store. Practicing Small Beginnings thinking, I immediately saw its potential and snatched it up for a mere fifty cents. At home, I put it in a basket (scavenged earlier and put away for just such a need) with a small container of toothpicks and a small container of large shiny beads. Voilà! A new exercise for Sophia, then three years old, who loved putting the toothpicks in the holes and then carefully covering each one with a colorful procession of beads. Great fun, but also great practice for her pincer grasp and ability to concentrate.

A few weeks later in a discount store I found some funny little toothpicks with clown heads on one end. I replaced the plain toothpicks and beads, and now Sophia had a new variation to capture her attention.

Anointed Shopping

My family calls this eye for interesting bargains *anointed shopping*. We laugh, but just as it is true that God supplies our needs, we can trust Him to help us find our teaching materials. If you are wondering whether or not you will be able to do this too, don't underestimate your ability. A friend of mine, who began "small beginnings thinking" after attending a workshop, looked for days without any success to find an hors d'oeuvres holder like mine. Then she made one out of clay, and now her children enjoy the same exercise.

God will give you ideas.

Small Beginnings thinking means quite simply embracing the principles and making them your own, then looking for new ways to apply them. I am so confident that you will think of new exercises that I hope you will share your new ideas with me. Maybe together we can fill a second book!

If you have sneaked a peek at the exercises that follow, you may already be starting a collection of pretty and potentially useful items to put together your own. But before presenting them to your children, one other area deserves our close attention.

To help our children get all they can from Small Beginnings, we follow a pattern designed to maximize the learning potential of each exercise.

Chapter Twelve

Working Together:
Presenting the Exercises

Now that you're on your way to putting together your own exercises, the only thing left is training in how to present them to your child. Both are equally important. The Small Beginnings exercises will have the maximum impact if you introduce them to your child following a few simple guidelines.

Above all, your child should be ready for and able to succeed at what you are presenting. Here is where your practice of observation will be of great service. You must know that he is capable of the necessary care, coordination, and movements. For example, is his pincer grasp strong enough to squeeze tweezers? Is his eye-hand coordination sharp enough to place a straight pin through the tiny hole in the center of a bead?

You will find a suggested age range in the following exercises. This is suggested only. Keep in mind that as young children, girls are sometimes as much as six months ahead of boys in development. Each child needs to be evaluated individually by the person who, as a result of careful observation, knows him best—you.

It is likewise important to go through an exercise each time it is presented to a different child, keeping that particular child's abilities in mind. Maybe this child needs a pair of easier-to-operate tongs. Maybe he needs something more challenging.

Although, as suggested before, you have probably already tried every component of the exercise to make sure it is child-friendly, practice the entire presentation several times before doing it with the child. Make sure every detail is covered and that the sequence is smooth. Take nothing for granted. Always put yourself in the child's place.

When the child, the exercise, and you are ready, the moment of learning begins.

Here is a procedure to follow:

1. Ask your child if he would like to learn how to use, for example, the smelling bottles. Show him where they are on the shelf.
2. If this is an early presentation, model careful procedure by using two hands to remove the basket from the shelf, walking slowly and quietly setting it on the table. If your child already understands the need for care, allow him to do this.
3. Sit beside your child and carefully remove the items arranging them as specified in the exercise.
4. Present the exercise slowly and quietly. Concentrate more than you need to. Keep your movements graceful and precise.
5. Avoid superfluous movements or mannerisms, as the child is sure to imitate them. (I once had a class full of children who tilted their heads to one side as they worked until I realized they were imitating me. I finally got my head on straight!)
6. As you present, observe your child's level of concentration. At the appropriate moment, invite him to continue or repeat the exercise.
7. Encourage your child to repeat, asking, "Do you want to

do it again?" Let him repeat as many times as he wants.

8. If your child does not perform the exercise perfectly, use discernment to decide if it is an important issue, then whether to re-present the exercise or to allow his variation.

9. Stay with your child as long as necessary, using your judgment to determine when he is able to work alone. For example, you would not leave a child with a bead exercise if you could not trust him not to stick them up his nose (yes, it happens). You know your child best.

10. When your child is completely finished, put the work away together and tell him he can now choose it any time he wants. An exception might be as in the case above. Then you might say, "When you want to get this work off the shelf, let me know, and we will do it together."

As your child uses the materials through the days to come, observe to see if they are bringing out his concentration, if he needs more of a challenge (smaller beads to tweeze, water to pour instead of rice).

The following exercises are not arranged by age, but are clustered by the type of emphasis. Some clusters are based on a progression from larger motor skills to smaller. For example, tongs precede tweezers, a baster precedes an eye-dropper. Read through all the exercises to find the ones that are age-appropriate for your child.

Now you're on your way, hopefully as eager to teach the Small Beginnings exercises as your children will be to learn them. Remember, the ones I've included are just a sample of what's possible. Using Small Beginnings principles, you may think of many more exercises to help release your child's potentials. And the presentation technique can be used to help your child get the most out of *any* learning materials you bring into your home.

Never lose sight of the goal: a self-reliant child who has a sense of order and can concentrate on a task; a child equipped to serve; a joyful child who loves to learn.

Be patient, take it one step at a time, may God bless your happy moments together!

Sorting

Materials in Tray

❦ Small container of buttons, five or six each of five different colors

❦ Five small dishes

Setup

❦ With child, carry tray to table.

❦ Remove everything from tray. Or keep everything on the tray—you decide in advance. The important thing is to demonstrate *how* the child should do the exercise.

❦ Set up materials left to right—container of buttons on left, smaller dishes on right.

Presentation

❦ Using pincer grasp, remove a button from the container and examine closely.

❦ Place in one dish.

❦ Remove second button and examine.

❦ Compare with button in the dish: If same color, put in dish also; if not, put in another dish.

❦ Remove third button, examine, and compare.

❦ Either place in dish with like kind or put in another dish.

❦ Continue sorting, inviting child to take over when the moment is right.

❦ When complete, examine all dishes to see that contents in each are the same. Correct any errors.

❦ Put all buttons back into common container and encourage child to sort again.

❦ Return materials to tray.

❦ Return tray to shelf.

Emphasis

❦ Slow and precise movements

❦ Left-to-right activity

❦ Concentration on careful matching

Foundational Value

❦ Eye-hand coordination
❦ Pincer grasp
❦ Development of concentration
❦ Development of visual discrimination

Remarks

By choosing buttons that differ not only in color, but size and texture, this can become a blindfold exercise as well, developing tactile discrimination.

❦ Any objects can be used for sorting: shells, different dried beans, marbles, etc. Other possible sorting containers include muffin tins and relish dishes.

❦ One of my children's favorite variations is using a small spoon to sort out marbles from a bowl into glass casters.

Age Range

❦ Two to four years

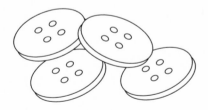

Wringing Sponge

Materials in Tray
- Two-compartment dog dish, water in one side
- Sponge, color coordinated and cut to fit

Setup
- With child, carry tray to table.
- Keep dish on tray, water on left.

Presentation
- Place sponge in full side, pressing down with finger-tips.
- Lift sponge with both hands and, without squeezing, move to right, positioning over center of empty side.
- Using both hands, wring sponge to release water.
- Return to left side and repeat until all water is in right compartment.
- Turn tray around to position water on left.
- Invite child to use sponge.
- Encourage child to repeat, turning tray with each emptying to keep water on left.
- As needed, demonstrate using sponge to clean up drips on tray.

Conclusion
- Mop up all spills on tray with sponge and give final wring.
- Return tray to shelf.

Emphasis
- Slow and precise movements
- Left-to-right activity
- Wringing all water out of sponge

Foundational Value
- Eye-hand coordination

- 🐞 Development of concentration
- 🐞 Strengthening of hand muscles
- 🐞 Preparation for reading (left to right)

Remarks

- 🐞 The challenge is learning the contrast between wringing the water out of the sponge and being careful not to squeeze as the sponge is moving between compartments.

Age Range

- 🐞 One and a half to three years

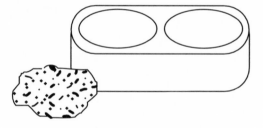

Spooning

Materials in Tray

- ❦ Two medium bowls, left one ¾ filled with dried beans, rice, or popcorn kernels
- ❦ Spoon

Setup

- ❦ With child, carry tray to table.
- ❦ Keep bowls on tray, full one on left.

Presentation

- ❦ Draw child's attention to contents of bowls, noticing one is full and one is empty.
- ❦ Demonstrate correct grasp of spoon.
- ❦ Carefully scoop spoonful of contents of left bowl and lift.
- ❦ Slowly bring spoon over, position over center of right bowl, and empty.
- ❦ When left bowl is empty, turn tray so that full bowl is on left.
- ❦ Invite child to spoon. If beans spill outside bowl, show how to pick up, using pincer grasp.
- ❦ Encourage repetition, turning tray after each, to pour left to right.

Conclusion

- ❦ Pick up any stray beans.
- ❦ Return tray to shelf.

Emphasis

- ❦ Left-to-right activity
- ❦ Careful movements to avoid spills
- ❦ Pincer grasp to pick up dropped beans

Foundational Value

- ❦ Eye-hand coordination

- ❦ Development of concentration
- ❦ Preparation for reading (left to right)
- ❦ Pincer grasp (picking up stray beans)

Remarks

- ❦ Much variation is possible by setting up exercises of different proportions. As child develops more coordination, use smaller bowls, beans, and spoons—even tiny egg cups filled with barley and a miniature spoon.

Age Range

- ❦ One and a half to three and a half years

Pouring

Materials in Tray

- ❦ Two small pitchers, creamer-sized, facing to center, left one ¾ filled with water
- ❦ Small sponge

Setup

- ❦ With child, carry tray to table.
- ❦ Keep pitchers on tray, full one on left.

Presentation

- ❦ Draw child's attention to contents of pitchers, noticing one is full and one is empty.
- ❦ Using pincer grasp, grasp handle of left pitcher, lift slowly, and move to right.
- ❦ Position carefully, so when pouring begins, spout will be lowered over center of right pitcher.
- ❦ Be dramatic. Pour slowly and carefully, watching the water carefully.
- ❦ When pitcher is drained, place carefully back on tray.
- ❦ Wipe up any drips with sponge.
- ❦ Turn tray, so filled pitcher is on left.
- ❦ Invite child to pour.
- ❦ Encourage repetition, each time turning tray to pour left to right.

Conclusion

- ❦ Mop up all spills with sponge.
- ❦ Return tray to shelf.

Emphasis

- ❦ Left-to-right activity
- ❦ Careful movements to avoid drips

Foundational Value

- ❦ Eye-hand coordination

❦ Development of concentration
❦ Preparation for reading (left to right)

Remarks

❦ Choose pitchers appropriate in size for the ability of your child. The smaller the pitcher, the more control will be required to pour without spilling.
❦ Begin younger children on pouring by filling pitchers with rice, barley, or birdseed.
❦ Advanced variation: one pitcher with four or five small cups (like a tea set). Fill pitcher with birdseed or water. The complication here is that the pitcher holds more than the first cup can hold, so the child must have the capacity to stop before the cup overflows.

Age Range

❦ Dry pouring = Two to three and a half years
❦ Water pouring = Three to five years

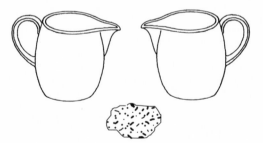

Basting

Materials in Tray

- 🐾 Two-compartment dog dish, water in one side
- 🐾 Baster
- 🐾 Small sponge

Setup

- 🐾 With child, carry tray to table.
- 🐾 Keep dish on tray, water on left.

Presentation

- 🐾 Demonstrate squeezing baster, then releasing.
- 🐾 Squeeze baster, then place in water.
- 🐾 Release slowly, drawing child's attention to water flowing up the baster.
- 🐾 Remove baster from left side and, without squeezing, move to right.
- 🐾 Squeeze baster to release water.
- 🐾 Return to left side and repeat until all water is in right compartment.
- 🐾 Turn tray around to position water on left. Invite child to baste.
- 🐾 Encourage child to repeat, turning tray with each emptying to keep water on left.
- 🐾 As needed, demonstrate using sponge to clean up drips and wringing over dish.

Conclusion

- 🐾 Mop up all spills with sponge and give final wring.
- 🐾 Return tray to shelf.

Emphasis

- 🐾 Slow and precise movements
- 🐾 Left to right activity
- 🐾 Squeezing and releasing baster

Foundational Value

- Eye-hand coordination
- Development of concentration
- Strengthening of hand muscles
- Preparation for reading (left to right)

Remarks

- Add a few drops of food coloring to the water to make it more conspicuous.
- Make a small sponge by cutting one in half.
- Squeezing the baster comes naturally to children. The challenge is in learning to release, to keep it underwater while releasing, and to move it without squeezing.

Age Range

- Two and a half to five years

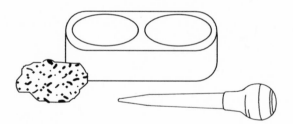

Eyedropper

Materials in Tray

- ❦ Two or more tiny jars or bottles, largest one ¾ filled with water
- ❦ Eyedropper
- ❦ Small sponge

Setup

- ❦ With child, carry tray to table.
- ❦ Remove everything from tray (or keep everything there—the important thing is to demonstrate *how* the child should do the exercise—you decide in advance).
- ❦ Set up materials left to right—full jar on left.

Presentation

- ❦ Demonstrate squeezing eyedropper, then releasing.
- ❦ Squeeze eyedropper, then place in full jar.
- ❦ Release slowly, drawing child's attention to water flowing up eyedropper.
- ❦ Remove eyedropper from jar and, without squeezing, move to jar on right.
- ❦ Squeeze dropper to release water.
- ❦ Return to left jar and repeat until all water is in jar on right.
- ❦ Change position of jars, putting full one on left. Invite child to continue.
- ❦ Encourage child to repeat, demonstrating use of sponge to clean up drips.

Conclusion

- ❦ Wipe up all drips.
- ❦ Return items to tray.
- ❦ Return tray to shelf.

Emphasis

- ❦ Slow and precise movements

- 🐾 Left to right activity
- 🐾 Pincer grasp

Foundational Value

- 🐾 Eye-hand coordination
- 🐾 Development of concentration
- 🐾 Fine motor control
- 🐾 Preparation for reading (left to right)

Remarks

- 🐾 Add a few drops of food coloring to the water to make it more conspicuous.
- 🐾 Make a tiny sponge by cutting one in eighths.
- 🐾 Squeezing the eyedropper is easy. The challenge for children is to transfer the full dropper from one bottle to another without squeezing.
- 🐾 This is a refinement of the basting exercise.

Age Range

- 🐾 Three to five years

Funnels

Materials in Tray

- A collection of small bottles or jars
- Small pitcher of water
- One or more funnels
- Small sponge

Setup

- With child, carry tray to table.
- Remove everything from tray (or keep everything there—the important thing is to demonstrate *how* the child should do the exercise—you decide in advance).
- Set up materials left to right—funnel on left.

Presentation

- Demonstrate placing funnel into mouth of bottle.
- Pour water very slowly from pitcher.
- Demonstrate watching carefully, in order to stop before bottle overflows (since the pitcher contains more water than the bottle can hold).
- Repeat, using a few variations with different bottles and funnels.
- Invite child to take over when appropriate.
- Encourage child to repeat, using as many variations as your setup allows, exploring the different capacities of the bottles.
- As needed, demonstrate using sponge to clean up drips and wringing over the pitcher.

Conclusion

- Mop up all spills with sponge and give final wring.
- Return materials to tray.
- Return tray to shelf.

Emphasis

- Slow and precise movements

- Left to right activity
- Careful observation to prevent overflows and spills

Foundational Value

- Eye-hand coordination
- Development of concentration
- Gross and fine motor control
- Early work in capacity and measurement

Remarks

- Add a few drops of food coloring to the water to make it more conspicuous.
- Make a smaller sponge by cutting kitchen one in quarters or eighths.
- For younger children, use sand and larger containers.
- For youngest or special needs children, use very large plastic box with layer of rice, plastic cups, and large funnels.

Age Range

- Four to seven years
- Begin at age two for rice variation, three for sand.

Tongs

Materials in Tray

- Plastic ice cube tray
- Plastic novelty ice cube shapes (available in summer), cotton balls, or any appropriate objects in an open container
- Tongs

Setup

- With child, carry tray to table.
- Remove items from tray, placing in left-to-right order: tongs, container of objects, ice cube tray.

Presentation

- Demonstrate correct grasp of tongs.
- Demonstrate opening and closing tongs.
- Slowly pick up object with tongs.
- Moving left to right, place object in section of ice cube tray.
- Continue, filling ice cube tray sections in left-to-right, top-to-bottom order.
- Invite child to continue.
- Upon completion, switch positions of the ice cube tray and container.
- Working left to right, demonstrate returning objects to container.
- Allow child to finish.
- Invite him to repeat.
- If child repeats, again switch positions of the container and ice cube tray.

Conclusion

- Return items to tray.
- Return tray to shelf.

Emphasis

- 🐛 Slow and careful movements
- 🐛 Left to right activity
- 🐛 Pincer grasp

Foundational Value

- 🐛 Eye-hand coordination
- 🐛 Development of concentration
- 🐛 Gross motor coordination
- 🐛 Preparation for reading (left to right)

Remarks

- 🐛 Start with spring-action tongs, as the scissor-type are too difficult for young children. Save those for a later, more challenging variation.
- 🐛 Do not make an issue of filling the ice cube tray sections in left-to-right order, but do model it yourself.
- 🐛 A later variation with plastic ice cube shapes is to teach pairing like colors or shapes.

Age Range

- 🐛 Three to four and a half years

Tweezing

Materials in Basket

- ❦ Rubber soap grip with suction cups
- ❦ Small beads in container
- ❦ Tweezers

Setup

- ❦ With child, carry basket to table.
- ❦ Remove items from basket, placing in left-to-right order: tweezers, container of beads, soap grip.
- ❦ Open container of beads and draw attention to them.

Presentation

- ❦ Demonstrate correct pincer grasp of tweezers.
- ❦ Demonstrate opening and closing tweezers.
- ❦ Carefully pick up bead with tweezers.
- ❦ Moving left to right, place bead on suction cup.
- ❦ Repeat for a few more beads.
- ❦ Invite child to continue.
- ❦ Upon completion, switch positions of the soap grip and container.
- ❦ Working left to right, demonstrate returning beads to container.
- ❦ Allow child to finish.
- ❦ Invite him to repeat.
- ❦ If child repeats, again switch positions of the container and soap grip.

Conclusion

- ❦ Return items to basket.
- ❦ Return basket to shelf.

Emphasis

- ❦ Slow and careful movements
- ❦ Left-to-right activity
- ❦ Pincer grasp

Foundational Value

- ❦ Eye-hand coordination
- ❦ Development of concentration
- ❦ Preparation for writing (pincer grasp)
- ❦ Preparation for reading (left to right)

Remarks

- ❦ This is a refinement of the tong exercise, focusing more on small motor coordination than on gross.
- ❦ Select the most beautiful beads and basket available. Children love the colors and the challenge.

Age Range

- ❦ Three and a half to six years

Pins and Beads

Materials in Basket

- Pin cushion
- Four to six small containers of different beads
- Container of long straight pins with ball end

Setup

- With child, carry basket to table.
- Remove items from basket, placing in left-to-right order: straight pins, containers of beads, pin cushion.

Presentation

- With right hand, demonstrate using pincer grasp to pick up ball end of straight pin.
- Show child that one end is sharp. Give caution: "We only stick these pins into the pin cushion."
- With left hand, use pincer grasp to pick up a bead and place it on the straight pin.
- Follow with a couple more beads, if desired.
- Push pin into pin cushion.
- Repeat, making different combinations.
- Invite child to continue.

Conclusion

- Return beads and pins to respective containers.
- Return basket to shelf.

Emphasis

- Slow and careful movements
- Left to right activity
- Pincer grasp

Foundational Value

- Eye-hand coordination
- Development of concentration
- Preparation for writing (pincer grasp)

❦ Preparation for reading (left to right)

Remarks

❦ A magnetic pin holder or a strip of magnetic tape will keep pins from going astray.

❦ This exercise is highly effective in developing concentration and focus in children.

❦ When the exercise is completed, the child has produced a unique design; therefore, I do not require my children to put it away immediately but allow them to save it to "show Daddy."

❦ Make it beautiful with a variety of beads, different shapes and colors (available at hobby and craft stores). Children love the colors and the challenge.

Age Range

❦ Three and a half to eight years

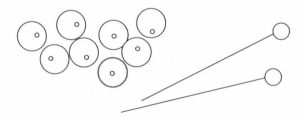

Sound Canisters

Materials in Basket

❦ Five pairs of 35mm film containers: two each half full of salt, dried beans, pennies, rice, water. Using sticker dots or acrylic paints, color code one of each pair with one color, the other with another color.

Setup

❦ Remove canisters from basket, placing all of one color in row on left, all of other color in row on right.

Presentation

❦ Pick up one canister from left row with left thumb on bottom and fingers on top. Do not surround canister with hand as that will muffle the sound.

❦ Shake by your left ear. Shake by child's ear.

❦ While maintaining canister in left hand, pick up one from right row in same manner with right thumb and fingers.

❦ One at a time, shake left canister by left ear, right canister by right ear.

❦ Shake each by child's ears, one at a time.

❦ If match is obtained, place two matching canisters in a pair off to the side.

❦ If not, maintaining left canister, set down right one and pick up new one.

❦ Shake each in the same manner, one at a time by your ears and by the child's ears.

❦ Continue until all matches are found.

❦ Mix up canisters and invite child to match.

❦ Stay with child through matching process, reminding him, when needed, of proper technique.

Conclusion

❦ Return items to basket.
❦ Return basket to shelf.

Emphasis

- ❦ Correct techniques so that sound is clear

Foundational Value

- ❦ Sound discrimination
- ❦ Development of concentration

Remarks

- ❦ This is a fairly complex sequence. The child's success is dependent on his ability to carry through exact actions, such as holding the canisters properly and shaking them by one ear at a time. You may need to point out that if he holds them improperly or shakes them simultaneously, he cannot hear their individual sounds.

Age Range

- ❦ Three and a half to six years

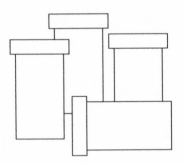

Smelling Bottles

Materials in Basket

- Five pairs of small containers (empty spice bottles are ideal, with both metal lids and plastic shaker tops)
- Cotton balls at bottom of jars are saturated with scents (e.g., clove, peppermint, vanilla)—two bottles per scent. Using permanent markers or stickers, color code one of each pair with one color, the other with another color.

Setup

- Remove bottles from basket, placing all of one color in row on left, all of other color in row on right.

Presentation

- Pick up one bottle from left row, remove top, and sniff. Let child smell too.
- Maintaining bottle in left hand, pick up one from right row in right hand, smell, and let child smell.
- If match is obtained, place two matching bottles in a pair off to the side.
- If not, maintaining left bottle, set down right one and pick up new one.
- Continue until all matches are found.
- Mix up bottles and invite child to match.
- Stay with child through matching process.

Conclusion

- Return bottles to basket.
- Return basket to shelf.

Emphasis

- Quick identification

Foundational Value

- Olfactory discrimination

🍒 Development of concentration

Remarks

🍒 This is a fun exercise, but must be done quickly, as the olfactory sense fades quickly. If this happens, put all the lids back on bottles and take a break.

🍒 Oils of peppermint, clove, etc., are available from health food stores.

Age Range

🍒 Four and a half to six years

Fabrics

Materials in Basket

- ❦ Ten or twelve 6" squares of fabric, two each of different contrasting textures (e.g., satin, corduroy, vinyl)
- ❦ Blindfold

Setup

- ❦ Remove fabric squares from basket, mixing all on carpet or table.

Presentation

- ❦ Put on blindfold.
- ❦ Pick up one square and feel it carefully.
- ❦ Holding square in left hand, pick up another in right. Feel for match.
- ❦ When match is found, place pair together off to the side.
- ❦ Continue until all squares are matched.
- ❦ Remove blindfold and check matches visually.
- ❦ Mix up squares and invite child to match.
- ❦ Stay with child through matching process, helping him, when necessary, to pick up fabric squares.

Conclusion

- ❦ Return fabric squares to box.
- ❦ Return box to shelf.

Emphasis

- ❦ Concentration on fingertips

Foundational Value

- ❦ Tactile discrimination
- ❦ Development of concentration

Remarks

- ❦ Younger children can do this exercise without the blindfold.

Age Range

- ❦ Four to six years

Chapter Thirteen

Notes from the Finish Line

In this book, we've looked at tried-and-true methods to bring out the best in our toddlers. By doing all we can to allow their God-given potential to be released, we will start them on a lifelong path to becoming the best they can be. And when each person in the family is on the same path, the home is better managed.

As a parent, you have probably already discovered (and you beginning parents will soon find out) that God has jam-packed our lives with lessons in character building. No, not theirs—*ours!* I can't think of any other aspect of my life that has caused me to become more conformed to the image of Christ or compelled me to cast all my cares upon Him.

Some people attribute my ability to handle a large family to my patience and serenity. The opposite is really true—my patience and serenity are actually a result of years of raising a big family. All seasoned parents stand as testimonies to the fact that our children change us.[1]

Sometimes we can be like children who balk and resist the process. How Tripp and I wish that we had reexamined our attitudes about sleep, for instance, before our fourth child. That would have saved us a lot of frustration. Instead, we muddled through many demanding nights—feedings, earaches, tummyaches, wet beds, bad dreams, sleepwalking—fighting for our right to eight hours' sleep or mourning the loss of it.

Somewhere along the line we decided we needed to change. Now, seven children later, our motto has become: "Sleep less, live more!" It's so much easier that way. We can be cheerful about any nighttime ache or mess if we never expected to sleep through the night in the first place.

Yes, some days I do feel more tired than I'd like. Still, I try not to let fatigue rob me of the reward of being a mom. Let's face it, for those of us raising toddlers, the days of plenty of rest seem too far off for our grocery-list-cluttered minds to imagine.

But when I catch a glimpse of my well-rested future, I can't help but think how much I will miss those peanut-buttered fingers tugging at my jeans. And no matter how long a particular day may seem now, I know I will remember them as going by too fast.

I've changed. I've learned that it's possible to be tired and happy at the same time.

Change is really what it's all about. Because as much as God requires of children to grow into all that He wants them to be, He requires more of us as parents. There are times when it hits me like a locomotive—the need to surrender—but with the Lord, surrender is always sweet. The more willing I become to let go of my own selfish desires—and learn to love my children as God loves me—the more joy I find in my days with my family.

Also, the more I understand God's plan for my children—in terms of the potentials He has given them for independence, order, self-control, concentration, and service—the more rewarding my job becomes.

We lay the foundation early in the child's life for how he will later approach his education, his work, his community, and his own family to come. And so the toddler years may be the most important years of all. But they can be the most trying as well.

If toddlers could tell us what they really need (not just what they want), you know they would—loud and clear. Since they can't, most people spend only a few years trying their best to understand them. Often by the time a mother figures out what makes her toddlers tick, she's graduated to helping kids with homework.

My situation is a little different: I've been over the track many times and even crossed the finish line a few. And I'm still running the race! One thing that keeps me going, and I trust will keep you going too, is astonishment at the tremendous gift entrusted to us in our toddlers. Surely we want to make the most of these years; and by understanding how to release their God-given potentials, we will.

But doesn't it take your breath away when you have a moment to pause and consider what it all means? The character we build into our children today will go beyond their lives to affect the generations to come. What an awesome privilege, what a great responsibility God has given us!

We just need to remember to take it one step at a time— beginning small.

Endnotes

❦

Part One: On Your Mark

1. I am convinced that our early years were not in vain. Like many who came to the Lord later in life, God's purposes were working themselves out so that all might be in place when the time came for us prodigals to use our talents for His service. I believe my early training was part of God's plan for my life. Therefore, if any wonder whether the Montessori method is compatible with Christianity, I would affirm the validity *only* of Maria Montessori's insights into childhood development and the techniques she developed to increase the child's capacity to learn. Most important, the ideas I share have been sifted through what I know to be true as a Christian and are compatible with our faith.

Chapter One

1. One of the most wonderful gifts God has given us is the ability to change. We do not need to fear, resist, or feel helpless when confronted with the need to change our behavior or our character. Especially when we have God to see us through the process. We can instill this positive attitude in our children from an early age by modeling it ourselves and by carefully walking them through the steps needed for successful change.

When you have identified a problem (whining, destructive behavior, carelessness, etc.), spend some time preparing for a special talk with your child. Find a quiet time to sit with him—sometime when you're not in the midst of correcting him for a specific incident. Then:

❦ Describe the problem: "Jamie, I've noticed that you've been taking things that don't belong to you and hiding them behind your bed. That is stealing."

❦ Discuss the moral basis: "It is wrong to steal. So wrong that God has a specific commandment against it. And Jesus said we must treat each other the way we would want to be treated ourselves. If Elizabeth took your special robot, you would be very upset. That's how others feel when they can't find their special things."

❦ Outline the consequences: "If you continue to steal, you will continue to hurt others. But most of all, it will hurt you, because sin separates us from God and makes us unhappy. When you stop stealing, you'll feel a difference. When we do the right thing, we feel God's peace."

❦ Ask for a commitment to change: "You can change. The first step is to make a decision. Are you willing to stop stealing?"

❦ End in prayer: "The Bible tells us that with God all things are possible. I know that's true because He's helped me with many changes I've needed in my life. Let's ask Him to help you. I know He will."

Here I have scripted an example of what to say to your child, but let him talk to you too. Sometimes bad habits or behavior are symptoms of deeper problems, and you will need to listen to your child to find out if there are other areas where he needs your help.

This process can be used from the age of three. Before that, the child does not have the cognitive ability to understand, that's why reasoning with a younger child is ineffective. By using this method, you will not only provide your child with solid help dealing with a here-and-now problem, you will also lay a foundation for his adult life of facing character problems squarely and seeking God's help to change.

Chapter Two

1. One Christmas tradition our children love is this: Every year, I buy each child a special ornament. Each child also has a storage box that will hold these along with others received as gifts through the years. As we admire their ornaments and help our children hang them on the tree, we remind them that these will be the beginning of their own family's collection, as they will take their collections with them when they marry. We also speak of the heritage they will carry with them of all that we have shared as a family. We have seen this completed in our daughter, Samantha, who married seven years ago and has carried on the tradition with her own children.

2. Tripp and I made a decision after our fourth child, Matthew, was born to leave our birth control to the Lord. We decided that if we could trust the Lord with other areas of our lives, then we could certainly trust Him in this one too. Recognizing that He has a plan for our family, we made a covenant to receive as many children as He thought we should have and not to worry—to count on Him as our Provider. Seven children later, Tripp and I rejoice that God has blessed us so abundantly and been so faithful. (If you are so inclined—but worry that you'll have eleven children too—just remember: God has a different plan for each family!)

Part Two: Get Set!

1. Down's syndrome is a condition occurring in one out of every eight hundred children, in which an extra chromosome is found on the twenty-first pair (hence the name, *Trisomy 21*). Though limited in intelligence, these children—especially when raised in loving, supportive homes—can grow to be actively contributing members of society, with their own unique gifts to offer. As the mom of three children with Down's syndrome

(one by birth, two by adoption), I know emphatically that Down's syndrome is not an unhappy ending, just the beginning of a different kind of story.

2. Our cultural notion of childhood "play" is mostly a notion. Once they have some mobility, children are more interested in the tools of living than in the playthings we give them. That's why if you keep your pots and pans where he can reach them, you'll find your toddler more often in the kitchen than in the family room.

Later, when language is in place, children do spend time with dolls and dollhouses, G. I. Joes and rocket ships; still, they are at work—sorting out relationships, adult activity, and ideas.

For the most part, a child is interested in doing what we do. He is interested in work. In fact, we could refer to this phase of observation, exploration, and imitation more accurately as work rather than play. Work is activity with a purpose, and the child brings an attitude of purpose to most of what he does.

Chapter Six

1. Parents just entering toddlerhood with their first may take heart from the fact that it is very possible for a child to "ask Jesus in his heart" at an early age. When that happens, Mom and Dad should see a noticeable change in behavior, and an even more dramatic difference in response to admonition. I know this firsthand from seeing the transformation in the lives of seven of my children as they came to the Lord. Currently, with four little ones, their daddy and I are teaching them about Jesus and preparing them to make a decision as soon as they are ready.

2. Independence has become a term with so many meanings to so many people that a few clarifying statements are necessary here. With toddlers, the drive to independence has the specific purpose of acquiring self-reliance skills. And while independence is a positive character quality, I must emphasize that in the healthy Christian individual there is a balance between independence (in terms of living skills), dependence on God, and interdependence on others. Thus, we do not encourage independence in children to the point that they lose sight of their need for God, their family, and—though to a lesser extent—their community.

Chapter Eight

1. Variations include walking with a glass filled to the brim with water or the old-fashioned book on the head. Try them, but with caution. For some reason, these tend to bring out the silliness in children; when water spills or the book falls, concentration is more readily broken.

2. We credit much of the peace and harmony in our home to the absence of television. Yes, it is possible to live without the tube! Our family has done it for fifteen years. The set we own is hooked up to a VCR so that we can watch movies or tapes our friends have given us of Sesame Street or the Olympics. Since our boys began playing Pop Warner football, my husband has also devised a way to hook up an antenna to watch the pro games.

Chapter Nine

1. A toddler discovering his will has an irresistible drive to exercise it. That's why the toddler years are often marked by tantrums and power struggles. Offering your child choices will provide opportunities for him to use his will within established limits. When this process is begun before the cycle of power struggles has set in, the child is not so prone to assert his will inappropriately.

Chapter Ten

1. I don't handle clutter well. As the day progresses and our house becomes strewn with toys and books, shoes and socks, I feel my anxiety level rise. That's why, several times a day, well before we've gotten to the chaos stage, I call to my children, "Ten-Minute Pickup!" That's a signal for everyone to drop what they're doing and scatter through the house, putting everything where it should be. By the way, though we call it a Ten-Minute Pickup, all of us know that we may be working twenty minutes—however long it takes to get the house in order and Mom's sanity restored.

Chapter Thirteen

1. One personal example of how our children changed us: Tripp and I were both sports *un*enthusiasts. Neither of us participated in, watched, read, or talked about sports of any kind. Amazingly, our first son revealed himself to be a jock from the age of six. We watched him warily, like some sort of stealth missile that had landed in our midst, as he signed on for baseball, basketball, swimming, and ultimately, football. At some point we gave in, realizing that as your child's talents are revealed to you, you need to help him invest them. Now, Tripp reads the sports page (the better to talk about what interests Joshua), and the whole family watches football. Lucky for us we gave in early, as we now have three other sons following in Joshua's footsteps—spending Pop Warner football season covered with bumps and bruises.

On the other hand, our eight-year-old Benjamin loves not only football, but musicals and opera. Since Tripp and I enjoy these too, the only change this required was for us to include Benjamin when we go.

Appendix A

❦

Resources: Books, Videos, and Conferences

Toddler Bible Stories:

Beers, V. Gilbert. *The Toddler's Bible*. Wheaton, Ill.: Victor Books, 1992.

Henley, Karyn. *The Beginner's Bible*. Sisters, Oreg.: Questar, 1990.

Lindvall, Ella K. *Read-Along Bible Stories* (volumes 1–3). Chicago: Moody, 1985.

Discipline:

Dobson, James. *The New Dare to Discipline*. Wheaton, Ill.: Tyndale, 1992.

Sears, William and Martha. *The Discipline Book*. New York: Little, Brown and Co., 1995.

Housecleaning:

Aslett, Don. *Is There Life after Housework?* Cleaning Center, Inc., Pocatello, Idaho, 1-800-451-2402, video, 1987.

Marriage and Parenting:

Christian Parenting Today magazine.

Crase, Dixie Ruth and Art Criscoe. *Parenting by Grace: Discipline and Spiritual Growth*. Nashville, Tenn.: Convention Press, 1992.

Fall Festival of Marriage, sponsored by the Sunday School Board of the Southern Baptist Convention, 1-800-254-2022.

Family Life Conferences, a ministry of Campus Crusade for Christ, 1-800-999-8663.

Morgan, Robert. *Empowered Parenting*. Nashville, Tenn.: Lifeway, 1996.

ParentLife magazine.

Appendix B

Age-Appropriate Chores

Each child has his own timetable, so ages are suggested and approximate. Ages given are on the early side; for boys, who mature more slowly, add up to six months to ages given.

1½ Years

- Getting diaper for self or new baby
- Putting disposable diaper in trash
- Picking up small items from floor
- Shutting cabinet doors
- Turning on dishwasher

2 Years

- Putting away toys
- Unloading dishwasher—putting away plastic dishes and cups

2½ Years

- "Folding" napkins
- Helping set table
- Putting away silverware
- Peeling carrots
- Pouring measured items into mixing bowl
- Putting away broom and dustpan

3 Years

- Dusting lower shelves
- Emptying small trash cans
- Carrying stacks of clothes to rooms

4 Years

- Feeding baby
- Putting away books
- Further dusting
- Sorting recyclables

5 Years

- Making bed
- Setting table
- General straightening of rooms

6 Years

- Pouring milk for family meals
- Clearing table
- General folding
- Polishing silver, brass

7 Years

- Vacuuming
- Loading dishwasher
- Sweeping floor
- Opening cans
- Cleaning windows

8 Years

- Washing pans
- Cleaning bathrooms
- Beginning cooking skills

9–10 Years

- Changing baby's diapers
- Further cooking skills
- At this age, the child should be able to learn any house-keeping skill, as long as you are willing to teach him.

Appendix C

❦

A Spoonful of Scripture

❦

Two are better than one,
because they have a good return for their work.
Ecclesiastes 4:9

❦

Commit to the LORD whatever you do, and your plans will succeed.
Proverbs 16:3

❦

Even a child is known for his actions,
by whether his conduct is pure and right.
Proverbs 20:11

❦

He who works his land will have abundant food,
but the one who chases fantasies will have his fill of poverty.
Proverbs 28:19

❦

Whatever you do, work at it with all your heart,
as working for the Lord, not for men.
Colossians 3:23

❦

Serve one another in love.
Galatians 5:13

❦

If anyone serves, he should do it with the strength God provides,
so that in all things God may be praised through Jesus Christ.
1 Peter 4:11

❦

A cheerful heart is good medicine.
Proverbs 17:22

❦

God loves a cheerful giver.
2 Corinthians 9:7

Postscript

❧

With this book complete, I find myself already excited about the next. In *Ready, Set, Read* I will focus on the miracle of language development in children—from the first spoken words to the first written ones.

Having taught scores of children how to read (as well as many parents how to teach them), I can show you how easy it really is to set your children on the road to reading and writing.

In addition, I will be reviewing the very best of children's books—secular, Christian, old, and new—with recommendations for appropriate ages and discussion ideas.

What keeps me going as a writer is thinking of you who will read this book and of your children. Which brings me to a special request: Would you send me a picture of your family? My dream is to paper the walls around my writing space, so that as I write I can be reminded of all of you.

You may sometimes be too busy to appreciate the adventure you have embarked on raising children. My greatest hope is to remind you how wonderful it really is.

Blessings to you,

Barbara

Please send letters and photos to:
Barbara Curtis
c/o Broadman & Holman
127 Ninth Avenue North
Nashville, TN 37234